THE WIT AND WISDOM
OF
DON A. JOHNSON

From his Journals 1940 – 1987

Compiled and edited by Byrne L. Johnson

THE WIT AND WISDOM OF DON A. JOHNSON
From His Journals 1940 – 1987

Compiled and edited by Byrne L. Johnson

The Wit and Wisdom of Don A. Johnson
From His Journals 1940 – 1987

Table of Contents

Introduction

In 1929 my father, Don Johnson, took the position of counselor/boatman/caretaker at Camp Kooch-i-ching, a private boys' camp on the Canadian border of Minnesota. He kept a journal for a couple of winter months in 1936 as he chronicled his progress in building a sailboat for the camp.

In the summer of 1936 he moved with his wife, Layna, and their three children to assume a similar position at Redcrest, the summer estate of Bror & Gilda Dahlberg. At Redcrest he only kept journals for a few months of 1940 and 1942 where he recorded some of his activities.

By November of 1944 the family made the decision to leave Dahlbergs, buy an island and establish a summer resort. He also picked up the journaling to record this transition.

Don continued recording in annual journals for the next 42 years with his final entry in August of 1987, by which time he was suffering quite severely with Parkinson's disease and found it very difficult to write legibly.

In 1990 I began to transcribe his journals to the computer as a way to make some of them more readily shared with my siblings, Buck, Sally and Karen, as well as other family and friends.

Not being a particularly good typist, I decided to start with the 1944-45 journals, knowing that that was an extremely important year in the life of the Johnson family. As I was doing the transcription, I came upon a number of unfavorable references to myself. There was a brief temptation to skip these parts, knowing that it was unlikely that anyone else would go back to read the handwritten copy once a printed copy was available. I did not give in to that temptation and included all of it.

Having finished the 1945 journal, I thought that I would pick another significant year and selected 1967, the year Don retired from the Boise Cascade Corporation. I then felt that in order to get a broad picture of his life I could do every five years so went to 1950. It didn't take long to realize that the other years were equally significant, so I started doing them all. By 2003 they were all transcribed, my daughter Etta did

1956, her birth year and Sally's daughter Nancy did 1981, a year that she had spent a significant part of the summer with her grandparents on Norway Island.

I created a computer file for each year and as a year was completed, it was printed and bound with a comb binding, shared with my siblings for their corrections and additions to be added as footnotes and then the file was corrected and reprinted. Besides doing cleanup, in that second pass through the journals I created a file of witty and wise short quotes that pleased me. This was a very subjective effort but hopefully it captured his humor, gift of words and understandings about life.

This material needed some organization other than chronology, so I sorted it into the categories listed on the title page. These categories are certainly arbitrary and subjective but hopefully will be helpful for the reader.

Enjoy!!

Byrne Johnson
Rainy Lake
January 2010

Chapter 1 – Cards & Sports

- *Don was a passionate Minnesota Twins baseball and Viking football fan. He also loved to play cards, sometimes for money but that was not at all important for his pleasure.*

10/30/48 Williams introduced us to game of "Red Dog". I came out $7.00 winner so think it a mighty fine game.

8/4/49 The gals took us pretty bad in cribbage which pleased them a lot more than it hurt us so everyone happy.

9/26/49 Ed & I took two guests for $1.00 in cribbage. Didn't actually cheat, but stretched honesty to breaking point. They died in stink hole 3 times. Once when they needed 17 to go out and took 16 for a 20 hand!

1/15/50 Layna doesn't lose those games any more gracefully than she did gin or cribbage - maybe because I "smirk" when I win

8/12/52 McKnight thot he could play cribbage and I took him for $3 before he changed his mind.

1/9/53 Beat Layna 3 straight in cribbage and somehow she did not seem to like it!

1/21/53 Lou and I won 3 straight. I am afraid that Layna & Cliff didn't share our pleasure.

6/26/53 Played 3 games of cribbage with Mr. Sprague and he made $.50 on me. You would think it was $50.00 the way he acted. It makes me feel good to do so much for the great man, but by God, I tried to win!

5/24/54 Meant to give money back but he beat me so bad in gin, and made such a fuss over it, that I never told.

12/27/54 [Bridge] I'm not sure if I care for it yet or not. It takes a lot of figuring and seems to be a great deal of difference of opinion with the experts.

1/15/55 Even in that great game of skill, it helps mightily to hold good cards.

6/11/56 I honestly think that those fellows never ran across two better losers - and by God they were good winners!

9/10/57 He beat me out of $3.00 playing cribbage which pleased him mightily and hurt me but little.

12/26/59 Dancing has sure killed our card playing - which is a step in the right direction. I suppose we will go back to it some day when we get too old to dance.

9/30/64 Much gin rummy and Gerry and I lost $1.00 to Harold May and Blaine Evans. There is no question in my mind but the best way to entertain most guests would be to let them win at cards. It sure makes them happy - almost as happy as we are when we beat them.

8/25/66 Once he laid his cards face up and said "What in hell can a man do with cards like that?" I answered "Play them, goddamn you, like the rest of us have to do!"

11/18/70 What a helluva complex has been built up in America. No win - no fun.

12/25/71 A sad day in Viking land. Well, it won't be the same for me if I watch anymore. Something like hunting game you can't eat.

2/6/72 I decided I was a perfect opponent for him. He had to extend himself to win but didn't have to suffer in losing.

8/30/72 On way home Layna said "Playing cards with Harry is like sending to Sears. You never get what you order!"

12/10/72 We lost 23 - 7 and it was no fluke. How in hell can a grown man get so worked up over something so unimportant?

2/1/75 Layna and Harry took all three and Bern and I said "S**t" in our most dignified manner.

10/23/76 Jim took it pretty hard but it was a great game for me for two reasons. I didn't get cold (feather jacket and parka took care of that) and I didn't have to pee.

9/3/78 A good game to watch. The first half preempted by coronation of new pope - on all stations. A bunch of mad fans - even some Catholics, I'll bet.

5/19/81 A rabid 15,700 fans cheered them on. A contest like that brings out the worst in some people and there were times when I would rather be classed with the animals.

9/23/84 Vikings 29 - Detroit 28. Twins 5 - Cleveland 1. It is more fun to watch when our boys are winning!

12/17/84 Les Steckles fired as Viking coach. In his one year he won 3 and lost 13. A real slaughter. He has 2 years to go on his contract at $150,000 a year. That should help ease the pain.

Chapter 2 - Entertainment

- *Reading was a great source of pleasure for Don. He read anything he could get his hands on and often had pithy comments on books and authors. Movies and stage plays were also favorite pastimes, although he apparently had more negative experiences with film than with plays or books.*

- *For a number of years Don and Layna were very involved in square dancing, which came to an end when the doctor decided that it may be too much of a strain on my mother's heart.*

4/22/49 [Icecapades] Biggest entertainment thrill of my life. Goose pimpled for two hours

12/4/50 Finished *The Sling and the Arrow*. A homosexual theme - very morbid, and I hope, far fetched. Borrowed it from Carol Keyes. She shouldn't read such crap. Layna read it too, but is too stable to let such junk upset her - not so sure of Carol.

2/7/51 Finished Frank Yerby's *Golden Hawk* Pretty fair adventure story. Much of it very improbable but good "pastime" reading.

2/11/51 Finished *Infinite Woman*. I liked it. Should read it again and try to get more of his philosophy now that I know the story. Probably won't.

3/23/53 ..saw Marilyn Monroe in *Niagara*. The ballyhoo boys have put her on top - I'm not sure she has the stuff to stay there.

2/2/55 I read an article recently on "Minor Ecstasies". This show [*Cinerama*] was certainly one and in a number of places bordered on a few "Majors".

3/22/55 The rare combination of a man who knows his subject matter and has a beautiful literary style. [Cousteau's *Silent World*]

5/9/55 Saw Jane Russell in *French Line*. Her last performance in front of me.

12/23/55 Finished Jack London's *Smoke Bellew*. It is London at his best - and worst.

1/29/57 Finished reading Cruises' *LaVerandrye*. A most excellent account. The trouble I have found in books of that nature is that the authors seldom have both style and knowledge of subject matter.

10/23/57 [*Ten Commandments*] DeMille sure used his imagination on that one. I can well see how he spent $10,000,000 on it, but feel he should have been working on a rocket to the moon instead.

12/7/58 Finished *World of Susie Wong*, the love story of a Chinese whore and an English artist. An exceptional book. Written in the first person. He brings out the fact that Susie is what she is mainly for one reason - she is illiterate. I do not mean the fact that she is a whore - rather because of her ability to judge people, events, things. Her judgment is not colored by years of reading other people's ideas and therefore stands on her own. It is a new angle, to me, at least.

4/8/60 I wish the *Time* writers would spend less time trying to show how clever they are with words and more on giving an honest review.

5/3/62 off to see *State Fair*. Came out of place thinking "That is my last movie."

12/30/62 A terrific job on the dancing, choreography, lighting, photography but I missed the main point - whatever it was.

9/20/64 To see *Cleopatra*, a 4 hour show. We were 40 minutes late. Could have been 2 hours as well.

9/28/66 Layna and I to see *Who's Afraid of Virginia Wolfe*. Some high powered acting by Burton and Taylor but I missed the point. Maybe there wasn't any.

3/2/67 Layna and I to see *Georgy*, a highly touted English film. It was good, but would have been better if we had understood the dialogue. Had it been in Spanish, I would have done as well.

6/1/68 to see *In Cold Blood*. A powerful picture. Not sure how good.

3/9/70 Sally, Layna and I to see *Midnight Cowboy*. I still think that sex, like square dancing should be a participating rather than a spectator sport.

4/8/70 I have been trying to read Coovers *Origin of the Brunists*. At times it is absolutely brilliant. Then it gets so far out that I can't follow. Mixed in with this there are many 4 letter words, many which add nothing to anything.

4/12/70 A very, very unusual book - and all in all I liked it - altho I thot Mr. Coover must have been hopped up when he wrote some of it.

4/21/70 We are getting a little "down" from this weather so went to see *La Dolce Vita*. What a goddamn farce. I vowed that those damned Dagos wouldn't suck me in on another deal like that.

1/17/71 The movie makers must believe that we Americans thrive on shock and dish it out in big doses. Crap!

2/23/71 We got seats in the enclosed area at the park and listened to the music(?) of two bands. The young ones were twisting hell out of themselves.

4/23/71 Finished reading Jack London's *Sea Wolf*. I can see why he was so popular in the '20's and '30's but won't sell now.

3/11/72 He learned to dance just to prove I didn't know what I was talking about. She says he still isn't too good! It was a fun gab fest, with the Davises doing about 2% of the listening.

3/26/72 Had a nap, ate dinner and to movie - *Dirty Harry*. What a bloody, obscene picture. Awful!

6/25/72 As Orm said to Gudermund, "I know you are a great man because you told me so yourself!" [*The Long Ships*]

11/19/74 Our movies have become so rotten that I would not have been surprised if they had shown Mr. Adams in bed with a she bear. [*Grizzly Adams*]

2/7/75 Lisa with us to "R" rated *Freebie and the Bean.* A blood and guts spectacular but not enough sex to be too objectionable. The language pretty rough but Lisa has heard Dad and Grandpa.

2/28/75 *Daily Journal* carried a front page story, with picture that showed Jean Manley presenting a PLAGUE(!) to a Shelly LaJambe. It doesn't take much to brighten my day.

4/17/75 The 14 singers in complete harmony. I had goose bumps on the goose bumps. I have been worried lately as to what has happened to my capacity to enjoy things. Now I know it is not completely gone. I was really thrilled tonight.

3/18/76 Home by 8:30 in time to go to movie, *Lucky Lady*. A so called comedy, full of sex and violence. Our senior citizen admission of $1.00 apiece was too much.

10/5/76 Buck and I to see *Midway*. Very impressive, not so much because of heroism shown by navy but by techniques that put in on film.

10/14/77 Times have changed to point where anything goes. We read the dirty book which a dirty movie followed closely.

1/29/78 Finished reading Frederick Manfred's *Milk of Wolves*. If he is not nuts, the rest of us are. I don't know what possessed me to finish the damned book. It got steadily worse - and no improvement at finish.

4/28/78 Finished reading John MacDonalds *Condominium*. A powerful book. Now I am really sure we will never move to Florida!

1/14/79 Read my 1958 diary. Some interesting reading mixed in with the trivia. Read Sunday paper from cover to cover. My diary more interesting.

1/21/80 Finished reading *Fools Die*. It held my attention through out. Don't think I would recommend it to someone else. The language was rotten.

2/5/80 Finished *The Navigator* - it died before the end!

10/30/80 A dirty picture! Senior citizens get a deal. We pay $3.00 apiece for 3 shows then get 4th one free. I seriously doubt if we will go to two more in order to get that free one.

1/22/81 We stopped at recreational building and watched square-dance caller put his 7 squares of dancers thru their paces. I only cried a little bit.

12/3/81 Started to read *Women's Room*. Got far enough in it to know that all men are chauvinist pigs and women are long suffering at their hands.

3/13/83 Tommy came with the paper and we put in the rest of the day reading the bad news.

4/2/84 To see opera *Don Pasquale*. It was done in English but it could have been in Chinese.

2/14/85 I read from *Elmer Gantry*. His character is developing slowly but now (where I am in book) he is already a #1 bastard.

11/7/85 We watched 3rd installment of *North and South*. We were a bit embarrassed during the lovemaking but the kids took it in their stride.

Chapter 3 - Fishing

- *In 1946 Don was hired by the Minnesota & Ontario Paper Company to be the Captain on their houseboat <u>Mando.</u> He continued on that job until retiring in 1967. Most of these quotes come from that experience.*

5/23/48 Stopped at bridge by game warden who, when he saw who we were, said "I'm sorry".

7/6/48 Still holds up my contention that Nobody knows nuttin' about fishing!

7/12/48 Neither had done it before so I had my hands full. I actually believe that Karl hoped that nothing would hit, as he felt inadequate for the situation.

6/5/49 When fishing is poor, they are grateful for any small snake that might liven things up. When fishing is good, they aren't happy - where are the <u>big</u> ones?

6/19/50 …and he caught two nice bass. Very scientific about it all - otherwise might have caught more!

4/2/51 Got my bill for share of "Operation Crappie" from Carl. $37.50. That does it! I can't afford to travel in that company.

6/24/51 Guides out in evening with flyrods and Gerry broke into the win column by landing 3 nice bass. He sure is enthusiastic. I firmly believe that the way to make a good guide is to make him a good fisherman, too. Then he can talk the language.

6/23/51 I have developed a deep respect (and affection) for the smallmouth over a period of years and it hurts me like all get out to see one jerked around with a bunch of gang hooks in his body.

8/8/51 Dr. Webb, like a lot of other people who have watched a good fly fisherman, thot he could do it himself in one easy lesson. I spent the morning with him, and altho he does fairly well already, I'll bet he thinks it was easier to learn to take out an appendix.

8/12/51 Same old story - too damned much slack line - result of poor stripping. We are sick from poor fishermen.

7/14/60 My next job was to take Mr. Sweatt and Lanny (12 year old) and give them a big evening of fly fishing. We might as well have been on an elephant hunt.

9/4/51 - and I caught a 5½# bass on my 3½ oz glass rod. Gee, am I proud! Said Hunt, "Why didn't you take me to that place?" Said I, "What the hell would you have done if you had been there!"

3/27/52 To Sportsmen's banquet - the first in 7 years - maybe the last. God but I get bored. They have everything in the world to do with, and end up a bunch of prattling children.

6/21/52 Fished with Galeen & Seng and could have caught many bass but pulled out of bass water after they caught 4 on plugs. I just can't stand to see a nice bass mauled around on 3 sets of gang hooks.

8/2/52 He caught 3 good bass on feathered minnow right in middle of day. I still know nothing about fish.

8/19/52 Said Olson -"Goddamn". Said Searl after the fish made a beautiful jump "He deserved to get away". Said I, "Olson, you must learn to lose a fish graciously!"

1/25/53 Much criticism of methods by Keyes who knew not a damned thing about it. Had fun watching a 10# trout look my minnow over with very slight interest.

7/11/53 Walleyes hitting fine but everyone bass conscious and can't appreciate them.

8/15/53 That kind of fishermen would rather make 10,000 casts with the hope of getting a bass than actually catch a nice mess of walleyes.

8/22/53 Out with Sweatt and Addison Lewis for bass in evening. By far and away the 2 poorest fly fishermen I have guided. Lewis so bad that even Sweatt shook his head!

8/24/53 she is catching on somewhat to the art of fly casting (not to be confused with fly _fishing_).

7/30/54 Somebody remarked that it cost $250 per day per rod and I said "Well, maybe we can all use the same rod!"

8/23/54 None of them took too kindly to my remarks when I said that from my observation, there were many, many good fishermen when the bass were hitting like mad but they weren't so hot when the fish slowed down.

8/24/54 The poor bastard. Even that much money couldn't catch him a few bass, which he wanted so desperately.

8/25/54 The one bright spot in this picture is the knowledge that a bass does not show preference to a bug cast by Ordway over one cast by Don Johnson.

8/26/54 A big discussion of fishing by Jim DiOnne, Paddy Orvalla, Buck, Byrne & myself. The man power wasted would have cut enough wood to last us a year.

7/4/55 When two men get fouled up they say in unison "Sorry, old fellow, my fault!". A husband & wife team says "Be more careful, damn it, you are spoiling my fishing!"

7/13/55 Said Buck "Gee, Dad, I thot the same thing but wouldn't dare say it even tho I was just as mad." Said I, "Maybe I wouldn't have 20 years ago, either."

8/15/55 Wind blowing hard enough to make things damned miserable for man (J.B. & Rogers) and beast (me).

8/20/55 Said he, "You don't learn without asking questions". Replied I, "You still don't learn if you don't remember the answers".

8/25/55 Same old story - a lot of difference between a good caster and a good fisherman.

8/31/55 There is no damned use trying to tell those fellows there is no damned use to do as they do.

9/18/55 Same old story. You either fish for bass, work your ass off with the paddle, or drag a minnow with the motor running. If you hit the bass you are a hero. If you fail you are a s**t.

5/19/56 Some idiot inquired, "Does Louie's boat always catch fish." The Goddamn fool was with Louie yesterday when they were completely blanked! Fishermen's memory!

6/19/56 We caught a couple of bass but I was more pleased with his remark "I used this fishing as an excuse to get out and talk alone with you, Don."

6/18/57 "OK, Don, take us to a place where you <u>KNOW</u> there are bass!" Christ - I <u>KNOW</u> that 500 fish saw their lures today. I can't help it if only 6 were in the mood to strike.

6/20/57 Two good guys. Damn poor fishermen.

7/9/57 For years, I have had fun with the idea that if and when I get reincarnated, I will come back as a 6# bass and drive the fishermen nuts.

6/20/59 Jim a miserable caster and I thot I was back at Camp Kooch-i-ching undoing back lashes.

7/7/59 Clint, without a particle of doubt, the most clumsy man I ever saw in a boat. He tried hard - at different times to send one or all of us unto the drink, but we survived his mightiest efforts.

7/21/59 What a goddamn imposition for such fishermen to waste my talents plus Rainy Lakes resources on a day like this.

8/21/59 Said Manley when he hooked first fish, "This, and Don Johnson's good company, is why I want to come back to *The Mando*."

8/3/62 Davey got a bit obnoxious concerning his fish so we knocked him down a peg or two. Convinced him that it was not his fish just because he caught it.

8/24/62 We did not set any records but finished up with 8 keeper bass - which was better than a kick in the rear with a frozen boot.

5/28/63 He even told Snowball he was putting minnow on wrong. Answered George "Maybe so, but watch this minnow catch fish!"

6/22/63 My hook scar by far the greatest conversation piece in some time. Frankly, many times in past, when bass fishing with J.B. and the going is rough, I have almost wished to get hooked so I could change miseries.

6/24/63 In at dark, mosquito bitten as all hell but as I figure the guests get stung at least 3 times to my one, it is quite bearable.

7/12/63 Burt did his damnedest to hook one of us, but we were too smart.

9/4/63 Nuts. We not only are supposed to find fish, we are supposed to work it so the right man catches them.

10/8/63 Goddamn it. We fish when we should be hunting an hunt when we should be fishing. We chase bass when we should be after walleyes & vice versa. Tomorrow we go to Trout River and really get frustrated looking at ducks.

6/4/64 "We could get better guides on this boat but where would you find one that will take this kind of crap day after day!"

7/4/64 The only way I could get J.B. to quit was to run into a swampy bay where the mosquitoes damn near carried us off.

7/17/64 What a gal she is! Says anything that comes into her head - much of it would make Ava Gardner blush. She got a great charge when she caught a rock bass about as long as her bait and I told her "There is a school of thot which says he was not trying to <u>eat</u> that bait."

5/22/65 His tackle box would equip a small town store, and he believed in giving every bait a chance.

7/22/65 Both damned fine people, both damned poor fly fishermen.

7/9/67 Finch did not know a spinning outfit from a telephone pole when we started but got along fairly well.

9/15/67 I am often reminded of my answer to Mr. Davis when he asked me what the number 1 requisite of a good guide was. "The ability to take bull s**t!"

1/19/68 Saw 4 porpoises playing in bay. Not so sure now that I want to be reincarnated as a small mouth bass. Maybe a porpoise has more fun.

4/10/69 He said they were caught on plastic black worms and was selling them like mad. How gullible can fishermen get? I almost bought a couple myself!

6/21/70 A full limit all around but many were small and found their way into the skillet at noon.

6/26/70 Very well pleased they were and Branstad now knows all the answers about bass fishing. I understand that kind of thinking in a kid like Brad but it is hard to reconcile in a grown man.

7/27/70 Fished in area where I had seen many, many bass caught. Many old fishing partners with me tonight, none better that the one I had with me [Harry Davey].

9/24/70 Even tho I stay retired for 35 more years, I can not possibly use up the fishing equipment I now have. Boise Cascade and ADM have been very, very good to me - not all of it with their consent.

3/7/71 A big breaker dashed up to my knees and on to my live box. It let my fish go and also washed my shrimp bait out to sea. It was a good finale.

5/14/71 Maybe, down deep, we are showing we are completely emancipated from fishing and fishermen by leaving Rainy Lake on opening day.

5/27/71 Our gear, from boat to minnow bucket, functioning perfectly.

7/9/71 I suppose I have had poorer fishing in my life but fortunately I can't remember when.

9/11/72 I still spend some of my time "wishing" a fish on somebody's hook. Well, it was my chief occupation for many years.

6/20/73 Back to Water narrows where E.L. caught 2 more good WE. Even the loons couldn't match her laughter.

7/1/73 During my 22 years on the *Mando* I surely paddled hundreds of miles. Was I a modern galley slave or companion to the high and mighty? Both, I would say now.

1/19/74 I bought $10.00 worth of books, one of them on walleyes, which amazed Laird who thought I should have written one.

6/1/74 I showed Layna how to use a feathered jig and she showed me how to catch fish

6/17/75 We tried several places and came home with a total of 10 walleyes - some mighty small. As Layna remarked, the fillets looked like split wieners.

8/30/75 My Rainy Lake fishing hit an all time low this morning. I put a fat night crawler on a Lindy Rig at 8:00 sharp. I dragged it for 1½ hours - undisturbed. I then put it on a Little Joe (same worm) for another ½ hour. I brought him home, showed him to Layna and flushed it down the kitchen sink.

5/17/79 In March, 1920, I was 14 years old and alone in our dark house and speared a 24# northern. Never been that excited over a fish since.

10/17/79 Kept at it for 2½ hours without a nibble. I took it very philosophically, making myself believe it was better to be out facing reality (it was a fine day) than to be home fantasizing over the fish I should be catching.

6/20/80 When fishing got tough on Buck Lake, my Uncle Emil (my mother's brother) said it was because my Dad was responsible! He caught too many. Well, it could have been true. He did his bit.

8/14/81 Fished at Garbage Island, never tried it before, and all we got was a bunch of snags. I think that the cans and other debris we dumped there in past years have come back to haunt me.

3/4/83 George gung-ho to go crappie fishing, in desperation he set a folding tent up in the living room. They (the crappies) weren't biting there, either.

3/7/84 We had poor fishing some of the time, even in the olden days.

6/10/81 Harry and I gave fish one more chance to get caught by us. They didn't take it.

Chapter 4 - Hunting

- *Don was an excellent deer and duck hunter. Although he did some duck hunting from the <u>Mando</u>, most of his duck hunting and all of his deer hunting was either done alone, with family or with friends.*

10/13/42 Took snap shot at 150# buck and blew his heart out. I was more surprised than he was.

10/25/42 Later Vic said "Can you imagine that S.O.B. standing knee deep in 30-30 shells and saying he hadn't seen the buck!"

10/28/42 Went to Major Robert's cabin and borrowed skiff - some craft. Went on up lake and set up house keeping in Dr. Edward's cabin - some shack. Laughed half the night in cabin. The floor sloped so much that Vic asked me to nail his ears to floor so that he could stay put.

10/1/51 I shot 14 mallards while George was thinking it over.

10/5/51 Opening day of American duck season - and I missed it! Poor old Talbot laid down in the harness and barely got up. One engine out. Well - no squawk, altho I sure felt badly about the ducks

9/28/52 We got 9 ducks, but it was a struggle. I could have done as well with Karen in the bow of the canoe with a sling shot!

9/28/50 "A wonderful day, one they can never take from us – and it didn't cost $700 either!" referring to Carl's trip.

10/27/53 Wayne is trying to make a duck hunter out of her and personally, I think it is one of his bigger projects.

11/18/54 Instead of continuing the drive, he cleaned out his deer and hit back toward camp with it. That wasn't my way of doing things, and I thot I had brought him up differently.

9/22/55 Opal broke 7 straight clay pigeons and I missed same number! By god, I can hit the ducks tho, you can't eat clay pigeons.

9/30/55 How in hell can anyone be so poor after all the hunting he has done?

10/13/55 I enjoyed the day, largely because I wasn't trolling for walleyes. Happiness sure is relative.

9/20/56 When I realized how badly our hunting was balled up I just sat back and enjoyed the weather and beautiful fall scenery. I have definitely mellowed and for the good of my soul and ulcers. Ten years ago I would have gone stark raving mad at seeing so many fat mallards get away.

10/28/56 When I came in to say I had seen a mole, Layna said "you should have brought it in for a mulligan." [Their one elk hunting trip in Montana where they got skunked.]

10/5/57 Bluebills are coming in and I resent this fishing something terrible.

10/6/57 Good Lord - my duck hunting is like snatching at the crumbs that fall from a poor man's table!

11/10/57 Back to Neil Point but deer had got discouraged by all of our shooting and left.

9/11/58 Wayne says that Opal is as nervous as a bride in anticipation. I suppose she should be - for the same reason. She knows she is going to get something, but not sure what it will be.

10/20/61 Our deal was all balled up but - I can't criticize - would have done the same damned thing myself!

11/29/63 What sort of a built in mechanism do they [ducks] have to differentiate a feeder from a hunter? I thoroly enjoy watching them, how come so much fun killing them? Will I ever give up the latter entirely? Maybe not, but it is a thot.

10/14/64 We have fought the goddamn weather since early August, now that it is all over, we are having butterfly weather for our duck hunters.

11/5/64 As I told Layna tonight, I wouldn't take $1000 to have missed the last 3 days and I would not give a dime to stay one more.

10/3/65 Well, they had plenty of time to talk without interruptions from ducks.

10/21/65 Three beaver were completely befuddled when they came out of their house to find 4 large, cork mallard decoys facing them.

9/18/67 I paddled at least 1/2 the time. I wonder how often in his life a white man let his Indian brother sit in the bow of a canoe while he shoved him thru the rice.

11/5/67 I don't bawl him out when he doesn't see a duck! It must be a happy switch for him to go with someone who can do some "shagging" without the nagging.

10/10/68 Said George "I don't shoot as well as I used to!" When I realized that I always considered him one of the worst I ever hunted with, it sounded rather strange.

10/23/68 Buck and I drove the south point and Jim knocked over a doe and fawn. I asked Jim when the last time was when someone drove a deer to him and he answered "Never".

10/30/69 We landed on a point and set up decoys - which ducks completely ignored.

10/31/70 Ducks refused to decoy. Don't blame them.

5/7/71 Two pair of mallards swam by, and seemed to know that I wasn't the blood thirsty Johnson of Sept. 15.

9/28/71 Rain, rain and more rain. Plenty of wind, too. At 3:30 we said "to hell with it" and came in. Despite weather I thoroly enjoyed my day with Gerry. Home to a hot drink, a good meal and back to normal. Don to Gerry, "Let's call it quits before it stops being fun!"

10/7/71 He flew from New York. I'll bet there are more ducks in Central Park than we have here.

10/8/71 Said he "I am with the Fish and Wildlife, I would like to check your bag". In unison, we replied "Ha, ha, ha - what bag?"

11/22/71 He can't see well enough to recognize an elephant in a parade.

2/18/72 George very optomistic. Not me. It takes more than water to attract ducks. This area nothing but cactus and sage brush.

10/3/72 Bern wanted her 3 ducks skinned. If I had to skin all the ones I shoot, I would quit hunting. What a damn wasteful mess!

11/4/72 He told me he had shot and crippled a fox. Now how about that for an old deerslayer?

10/29/73 The 30 ducks that the Rahms have been feeding all summer were gathered around Buck's dock to see me off. I invited them to NWI but none showed up while I was there.

11/23/73 We could use the meat but what is more important, it looks like I'll go by my 67th year without a deer. Brace up, old man, it could be worse. You might be too feeble to hunt at all.

12/31/73 Somehow it seems a relief that the pressure is off, like a ball team breaking a long string of victories. I won't stop hunting as long as I can walk but from now on I won't have the feeling "I must not fail!" Maybe I can watch the squirrels and nuthatches more.

11/9/74 A doe showed up. In my trigger happy state I shot at her head. A lucky miss!

11/13/74 Thus endeth the poorest hunting season since 1918 when I shot my first deer. 2 partridge, a dozen ducks, no deer. I am discouraged but not disconsolate.

11/16/74 The "No hunting, cutting or trapping" signs on Deer Island keep everyone off but the Johnsons.

10/1/75 No one fired a shot! As I suspected, we had nothing to offer a passing goose other than a dumb looking decoy.

10/16/75 Not one damn shot at a goose. I took it all very philosophically - a box of super goose shells cost $8.50. The farmer charged us $5.00 for use of the blind. I reasoned that it didn't take all day of not shooting to save enough on shells to pay for the blind!

10/17/75 For years I have said that square dancing, sex and hunting are poor spectator sports. Today I changed my mind on the last.

10/13/76 I called Wayne to report. I think he was pleased to know that we got skunked - without his help.

1/7/77 A good letter from George Ray. He gave, in writing, to Cliff and me, exclusive hunting rights on Fawn Island. Everything from mice to moose. What a guy.

9/21/77 An interesting experience when I decided to butcher 4 of our ducks. Had them all lined up on raft when a man came around point in a motor driven canoe. First boat all day! I postponed the execution.

11/18/77 It must have been the brandy talking because I agreed to go hunting with Erle at 6:00 a.m. tomorrow. Snow almost up to "ass of 11 foot Indian".

7/27/78 The rabbits have developed a tremendous appetite for our flowers - daisies and petunias. Layna in a dither trying to chase them out of beds. I knew a better way. 4 shots from .22 and four rabbits in freezer.

1/4/78 Already Harriet thinks we are doing something wrong. Erle confides in me that she, in her partridge hunting, has scared all the deer out of their land. He doesn't dare tell her that.

5/3/79 I reminded them that they were eating the end results of my 1978 hunting season. 4 tame rabbits, shot with a .22. How far the mighty has fallen!

11/23/80 Well, I shot my share of all local game - deer, ducks, partridge, rabbits - and even moose. Memories, memories, few people can match mine.

10/10/81 I have mentioned the fact that I am not blood-thirsty anymore. I believe it. There was no desire to add that deer to the list of hundreds already there.

4/5/84 We hashed over a couple of hunting trips and Gerald wound up by saying, "I learned more about deer hunting those 2 times we were together than all the rest of my life put together."

Chapter 5 - Guests

- *Although much of the life on the Mando, as at Norway Island Camp revolved around fishing, many other relationships with the guests were worthy of note.*

6/10/45 Men seemed well pleased. A significant remark by one "There is as much of a change coming from Island View to here as there was in coming from Minneapolis to Island View!". Sure sounded good.

6/22/48 He was drunk the full time of party - and agreeably so. Never obnoxious, always willing to do as told.

8/2/49 Narrowly avoided a blow-up with Walter when I talked Mr. Davis out of wanting crappies for dinner. God damn these mixed parties. I feel like I am on a powder keg all the time. And foolish questions-worse that the kids at Camp. Mrs. Davis doing better. I am getting to genuinely like her. Watch out Johnson, don't get complacent.

6/11/50 Wrote letter to Gilfillan which I thought pretty good. Kissed him goodbye without kissing his butt. Let the old bastard find another place like ours if he can!

7/8/50 Downing an unforgettable character in that he is absolutely colorless - an unusual trait for *Mando* guests.

5/12/51 An interesting thing to watch Louise watch Lardy who is watching Louise so he can snitch a drink once in a while. He is rather good at it - as his condition testifies at times.

5/13/51 An interesting group of people. Men all up from bottom of ladder and now near top - and show it - especially Lardy. Women still pretty much small fry - but damned nice. It must be the contacts that polish the men - like me!

6/4/51 Joe Osborne, a repeat from last year, one of the few All American horses asses in *Mando* history.

9/5/51 John Gilfillan (the old fart) rode home with me in the Talbot. He brought a box of candy for Sally, and when it took him at least five minutes to kiss her the first time Layna said, "Gee, I was worried about you John, I couldn't believe you had aged that much in one year!"

9/9/51 MacFarland having a wonderful time. It has been a long time since anyone affected me like he has. He has been paralyzed from his waist down since 1932 and is most cheerful about the whole thing. I am afraid that if I had to face what he has gone thru, I would take the easy way out. Right now, I feel that I will never squawk about anything again.

6/5/52 A good lesson in public relations, but no normal person could follow it.

6/9/52 The world is full of people who ball up their lives with an over exalted opinion of their own importance. This outfit would have got along fine without me.

6/23/52 He must have something on the ball to have become executive vice president, but what ever it is, he keeps hidden from me.

6/24/52 There is no way of pleasing some people - and a few dollars bet will knock hell out of their perspective.

7/11/52 My belly, which was half full of mankind in general, damn near burst with this outfit. Damn the Sarvellas and I'll vote Republican if for no other reason than to "throw the rascals out!"

7/18/52 Shirley Faegre on modern education "You have to show the little bastards a good time or they can't learn anything!"

7/25/52 Well, to hell with that. We have handled bigger shots than he without any ass kissing.

8/16/52 Mr. Davis told me once that there was a liberal education to be had by listening to the conversation that passed across our table, and it is parties like this that make his words come true.

8/25/52 A most interesting thing how these parties vary from week to week. They certainly aren't standardized - and a good thing. It is just like fishing -unpredictable, therefore charming.

9/13/52 There are a number of men that furnish me a genuine glow when I meet them and these two are in the upper ten. If it were not for these contacts, this job wouldn't be worth a damn.

6/19/53 Incidentally, he is the only M&O employee (upper bracket) that has absolutely nothing on the ball that I can detect.

7/10/53 "Darling, divine, superb, plebian", etc., etc. $2.00 words flowing like water. Same old crap but on a higher plane.

7/23/53 she may develop into the same kind of a bitch as Gilda. Looks like the tycoons have a bum taste for women! Makes a bum like me most happy over the choice I made.

7/2/55 If I took the 5 finest people I know and took their best attributes to make one character, I would have Elmer Smith.

5/31/56 We play no favorites and everyone who lands here is an important person.

6/8/56 a garrulous old hypochondriac in my boat. Jim Edwards a sympathetic listener which helped. He carried at least 1/2 of the burden of hearing all about - what the hell did he say anyhow?

6/10/56 A most interesting talker on many subjects. We could listen now that Woodward is gone.

6/22/56 They are unique guests in that they are either playing gin rummy (1 cent a point) or talking business. I can't afford either.

7/12/56 The former one of the finest men I know. The latter a big mouth who is always sticking his foot into it.

7/16/56 A high class man despite the fact that he is a politician.

7/17/56 A long discussion with Bob on the evils of rotten language. Also the tendency of most men to let themselves fall apart physically at an early age. He said he admired the way I took care of myself - which made me tighten my belt.

7/25/56 Still think I am right, even tho my approach is bad.

8/1/56 Ed and I did our best to further confuse minds already a bit muddled.

8/9/56 I can't help but feel that our economics structure is a bit askew when men like these make so damned much more money than I do, and besides - their women aren't near as smart nor charming as mine!

9/1/56 I don't throw my weight around often on this job but it sure gives me deep satisfaction when I do. Maybe I should do it more often, just to let off steam.

9/26/56 Mr. Faegre and I out for 3 hours without a rise He was most agreeable. "Don, I have wanted to ask you something for some time. How much schooling have you had?" When I told him he said, "You are one of the best educated men I have ever known." I told him that much of it had been picked up at the *Mando* table, which I firmly believe.

10/4/56 "I am positive that you're wrong, but not sure enough to bet!"

10/7/56 Too late to do anything altho plenty of time to drink. I went to bed early.

5/20/57 Gerry and I took pictures of last years party and tried to match names. Many of the men seemed to step right out of the pictures and say "Hello". Others we both swore must have been superimposed because neither of us had ever seen them before.

6/8/57 I finally figured Joe out. He is just plain dumb - which he can't help. I don't resent him any more.

7/7/57 A death of a 90 year old great aunt who they were relieved to lose.

7/8/57 Said Mrs. Piper, "Captain Don, isn't this unusual, everyone talking and no one listening?" Said I, "What the hell is unusual about that?"

8/12/57 Insincere bull began flowing immediately.

6/21/58 I am sure the company would operate more efficiently if they would let the *Mando* crew prepare an "executive evaluation" of each of the boys who come up here as hosts.

9/29/58 As Gerry says, "This must be a good party to set so well with the crew so late in the season".

8/28/59 He [General Tooey Spaatz] was kidding me about me being handicapped by not having read *Book of Strategy*, like he had. I then replied, "Apparently you have already forgotten the first chapter which told you to never underestimate an opponent."

11/19/59 He closed his discourse by saying "There is not a single person in the whole damned company - with the exception of the two Faegres who could come into this club and meet the people, and create the impression, as you have done today".

5/27/60 I gave him the Gerry ulcers, Louie's heart attack, bridge tender heart attack routine, and altho I didn't impress him - he wasn't listening - it made me feel better!

6/14/60 My belly soon fills with his company.

7/5/60 The poor bastard cried so on my shoulder that I had to change shirts before going home.

10/11/60 So many interesting people on this trip and I had to listen to his bull.

12/16/61 He was driving himself so he could forget Mary. I didn't need that. I enjoyed thinking of her.

2/1/62 It has been an exhilarating experience for me to watch the workings of his agile mind.

8/8/62 I try to like him but it takes effort on my part.

8/31/62 He is the only obviously cocky guy I have ever liked.

5/8/63 MacKellar and Williams flew up to see us, not because they were worried but because they were thirsty.

6/9/63 Can't tell if he is a genius or a damned fool. No doubt it is somewhere in between, but I have not discovered the niche yet.

9/23/63 Gunderson, of Ashland, a bit obnoxious about it all. Said he, "There are fewer s**t heels in Ashland than here" and I replied, "at the moment - yes!"

10/10/63 Held myself in with an effort saying "are these questions as dumb as they sound or am I just getting fed up with whole deal?"

11/3/63 Said Shirley about P.B. - "He is a p***k!". She is so damned frank that I feel she must like us or would tell us otherwise.

6/4/64 They can call it the competitive American spirit that made our country great but by God, I have another name for it and it is spelled GREED.

7/16/64 Clint the clumsiest mortal on earth. He successfully knocked over my drink and Bob Faegre's at the same time. It took both elbows - but he made it.

7/20/64 They seem like good people, even tho they associate with Mabes.

7/20/64 The two women sat behind me and talked constantly for the 1½ hour trip. 90% of the time they were in unison. The roar of the motors saved me from trying to get the gist of the conversation - if there was one.

7/25/64 Either other people greatly overestimate my talents or I greatly underestimate them.

8/22/64 He said later "That was the best ride I ever had on Rainy Lake. How I wish Mary could have been here to be with us!" I damned near cried. Poor bastard, he will never get over that loss. It is the reason he drives himself (and us) so hard. What a helluva way to end out a life, living with the dead!

9/25/64 Said Ray Bowen "You people living here don't realize just what you have." I answered 'For Christ's sake, do you think I live in this country the year around just to see you once a year!"

7/20/65 There is no way for me to judge this man's ability as an administrator but I do hereby state flat footedly he appears to be one of the finest men I have ever met.

8/7/65 And we criticize Art Lee - and all Indians because they can't handle the stuff.

6/20/66 A typical question, asked at dinner table, "Don, when does the blueberry season open?" I told him "July 14, at 7:00 a.m.."

9/16/66 I am getting more and more resentful of the big shots - especially when they talk in millions of dollars and pass it out in tens of cents.

3/26/67 I am sure the rest agreed with Mrs. Campbell when she said "Shirley, there is something worse than loneliness!".

9/23/68 A warm day and they all are laughing about all the foul weather gear they have with them. I told them not to sell any of it until they see.

7/14/69 These people have no sense of punctuality and are late for meals - always. It drives Bernice buggy because she knows they are here for only one reason - to pester her. Wish I could feel that important.

8/10/69 Fred Olson told guests he had hunted with me 30 years ago. I did not tell the details of what an ass he made of himself at Lawrence Olson's place on Cranberry Bay. I must be mellowing.

3/8/70 Everyone had tears of regret when *Mando* was mentioned. Well, the truth is that they, the Faegres, fumbled the ball and Boise picked it up and ran for a touchdown. No fumble and we would all be enjoying the houseboat.

5/20/70 He raves about it like Hoppe used to rave about the houseboat - consequently, I am forced to doubt his sincerity.

7/15/70 Hattie Bliss now ranks #1 in the gushy gal category. She bubbles over at the smallest stimulus. Don't think she would wear too well on a long haul.

8/5/70 This party of 9 all strangers. When they leave they will still be strangers. We see little of them. They come down for breakfast, get in boat and gone all day.

8/6/70 Christ, but we have to put up with some damned irritating little pieces of crap.

8/14/70 Erv in a cast iron tizzy hoping that all goes well for the great man who is less than half his size.

8/14/70 They all seemed to agree that our economy is damned shaky and many businesses on, or about to go on rocks. Andreas apparently right there willing to grab the sinking ones at a ridiculously low fee. It reminds me of the buzzards along the road in Mexico waiting for a truck hit burro to make his last gallant gasp.

9/2/70 As I told Layna, we hitched our wagon to three wrong stars - Sprague, Faegre and now John Daniels. Well, it was great while it lasted in all three cases. We have no regrets.

8/15/71 The best indication of the volume of humanity is the fact that they almost filled the pot in the outhouse - not counting what was deposited in the flush jobs up the hill.

Chapter 6 - Family

- *The family was always very important to Don. He was often frustrated by Karen and Byrne, but never gave up hope.*

5/27/45 After supper, Buck went out in canoe alone. Went to bed early. Was still awake when we could hear Buck coming home in canoe - singing. By god, I couldn't take it any more and bawled like a baby! [Buck left the next day for the army.]

8/26/45 Had another row with Byrne. Don't seem to know how to handle him.

12/20/47 I stayed home alone and took care of Karen. Finally changed a diaper on one of our kids - and it was a dishtowel - all I could find!

2/20/49 To town in morning to pick up Sally. Very interesting discussion on sex - and quite startling. Olive enjoying ill health! Interesting discussion on sex! Layna "Guess I'm more animal than you!"

3/12/49 Big laugh all around when I spilled paint can over my shirt and Karen said "You sure are a helluva mess!"

11/27/49 For darn sure he [Byrne] isn't as cocky - must have got some of that knocked out of him last winter - so year wasn't a complete loss.

12/10/49 Karen wanted to get in drawer of table where I am sitting writing this. "Daddy, please move your little old belly so I can get some paper"! What a kid!!

12/20/49 Byrne's birthday. 20 years old, and still a ship without a sail. So far can get no answer as to his miserable showing at school last year or anything else. Might as well talk to Klinker!

1/14/50 It is most fortunate that I can say "we" in a case like that. Sure would be hell if Layna got big ideas from her association with wealth and splendor.

4/13/50 Karen said "That's right, Byrne, you tell 'em!" Discussion called because of laughter.

7/21/50 They say every man is entitled to one good woman and one good dog - I have had both.

12/2/50 She said we had received a D on the paragraph I wrote for her in English. I told her it was too deep for the teacher, which was a bad mistake on our part!

12/21/50 Our family all together tonight. Buck the least at ease - probably thinking about Dale, which is natural. The development of our family, like many others, has been an interesting phenomenon, and I would be blind not to see that this is the last meeting of it as such. Buck has his own now, and 2000 miles west. Byrne has 4 years in the navy which means he won't have an active part. Sally's will be gone at least 9 months a year to school unless she marries and makes a permanent arrangement. Karen is all we have left - which is normal. I have few regrets where the others are concerned. We may have fumbled the ball occasionally but all in all they are a damned fine lot.

1/21/51 Ma in best of health and spirits. Thoroly enjoyed visit with her. Altho she didn't say it in so many words, there is no doubt in Layna's or my mind, that she is worried over possibility of Catholics moving in on her on her death bed, when she is too weak to resist. We assured her that no such thing could happen as long as we are around, and she seemed satisfied!

2/3/51 Wrote what I thought was a good birthday letter to Sally. I certainly feel close to anyone I am writing to. Too bad I can't get myself to do it more often.

6/22/51 Ivy and Bud stopped in with another couple. I resented interruption and I'm afraid I wasn't too cordial. Didn't snub them by any means, but didn't go all out to entertain them like I used to do.

8/15/51 Started to paint house with Johnny Minter. He is the slowest damned kid I ever saw. Can't tell if it is a case of retarded development or what. He's far worse than Byrne was at his age.

12/25/53 Sally home at noon - and so happy! Flashes a ring from Jim. God, what a lucky guy to get a girl like that to love him so. I should know.

12/28/53 Jim came in on bus from Duluth. I keep wondering if he realizes how damned lucky he is!

12/31/53 I am neither happy nor sad over Sally's choice of a husband. He looks to be more than 50% right now so I have every reason to believe he will develop into something much better.

2/12/54 The feeling that exists between Sally & Jim and Byrne & Jane is most thin when compared with the love Layna and I have for each other. May the years weld them together with bonds of mutual admiration and respect as it has in our case - AMEN!

2/22/54 Left me alone with my work and thots - they interfered with one another. …. Layna had summed it up in her usual to the point language. "I told Sally that sex wasn't something you could turn on and off like a water faucet!"

2/27/54 I am not one to read between the lines on a deal like this. There is no need. It is right <u>on</u> the line.

5/1/54 Dale has been with us for 3 weeks. In that time she has said not a word nor made a single move which would in any way irk either Layna or myself. When her time came, she calmly called Layna and was off for the hospital. A champion for sure.

1/4/55 I fully realize that if Layna could master our finances along with all her other attributes, she would be perfection itself which has never been attained in modern times.

1/18/55 "Man's mind is forever ranging, he thinks he's improving as long as he's changing". E.B. White was right.

9/18/56 Spent $31.00 of my money for stuff for *Mando* crew. They take a lot for granted, which is all right. I raised them that way - just like our kids.

3/11/57 I called my mother and she said all was forgiven, tho God knows what there was to forgive. I have put this experience down as a prelude of what to expect as she grows older.

3/26/57 Buck & Dale here with kids to do washing. Buck gets as mad at his as I did at ours!

4/7/58 What a job to teach an 85 year old gal how to turn 7 buttons in the right direction.

9/16/58 I did my usual stumbling around for a present for Layna and came up with a small radio for her sewing center. I have done worse.

11/12/58 They were watching television and therefore we were not allowed to say a word.

11/10/59 Good to live with same old gal for 34 years and still be able to find something to say. I know many women who would drive me speechless in 34 hours.

4/16/60 My wife did not approve and attempted to squelch me by saying "Will you never grow up?"

2/5/61 Timmy fell into water thawed by our fire and when the rest of us howled, he said "Go ahead and laugh, it didn't hurt one bit!"

Timmy "Will anybody help me pee - NO!"

12/29/61 I finally decided that I had dilly dallied enough on this deal and came right out and told her it was the sexual angle and no other - which concerned me. I went into full details, which is something I never did with the other 3 kids. Don't know how it went but at any rate, we went to bed on a friendly basis.

P.S. What a level headed, clear thinking teenager we have. If she can keep her emotions in control, we have nothing to fear - but for how long says Grandpa Voice of Experience?

2/4/63 Sally's birthday - and we talked to her on phone. They are thrilled over new baby. How lucky can an orphan get? [Sally and Jim adopted three children.]

10/11/63 Of all the boys she has gone out with, he is the one I would like least for a son-in-law. Don't even know why I wrote that.

12/18/63 Many, many wise cracks, mostly aimed at Karen, but she got even as guests were leaving and Carey said "See the coat I gave my wife for Xmas" and Karen said "What year?"

12/22/63 I asked him to take me to Ranier and Layna said "why don't you get me one of those Eskimo carvings for Xmas?" Damn it - I blew up! I haven't gotten her anything that could be considered a sentimental gift for years and now this one won't be a surprise either

2/14/64 When she came in I made a couple of remarks that bugged her. She snapped at me so I calmly went to bed. Oh, to Hell with it!

6/16/64 She says she is learning what the suburbanites escape from when they come to NWI.

12/14/64 Layna came about noon. I could see her coming down the hall 100 feet away. I got the same thrill I used to get when meeting her in H.J.C. corridors in 1925. It must be love.

2/11/65 Home at 2:00. The house was cold because one burner on furnace out. I crawled in with Layna and we spent a short, restless night. Once I laid perfectly still with a cramped arm because I did not wish to awaken her. When my arm felt it was going to fall off, I moved slightly, Layna stirred and said "I have been in a cramped position for a half hour for fear of waking you". It must be love!

3/24/65 He is chasing Karen in a puppy like manner.

9/21/65 It was with mixed emotions that we looked for him. Much like when Buck, Byrne and Sally were missing at Camp. "If I catch them, I'll beat hell out of them but what if they have drowned?"

2/13/66 They have reached the point, at their early age, of looking right back at her as if to say, "Please finish so I can get at doing what I was doing and you are yelling about."

2/12/66 Jane taking a course in Orchestration at UMD. She tried to explain that in a 15 minute lecture that should have been delivered to the cat. He would have understood it as well.

2/15/66 Either she is conscience stricken at the thought of leaving me, or horror stricken at what her home will look like after three weeks of my housekeeping.

10/16/66 I am sure that Layna and I are closer than ever before in our lives. Forty years together and the bond gets stronger. Time will break it one way or another, but it is a powerful thing at the moment.

11/26/66 Jim showed pictures for about an hour. Good. He is proud of his kids as the pictures show. What lucky little ones to find their way into that home.

3/25/67 I find it easy to get philosophical and detect in these four innocent children the basic human traits that have so strongly contributed toward putting the world in the helluva mess it is in. Selfishness is possibly #1.

8/13/67 As always, I was not comfortable at the Edwardses - and as always can't explain exactly why. Certainly I resent the way they treat Gil. Maybe my old Scandinavian background demands more respect from kids.

11/22/67 We had a good visit, much of it concerning the raising of kids. She knows more about it now than she ever will. Great discussion on kid raising between Byrne and Karen in evening. Much talking and little listening.

6/20/68 Robin's sister and her preacher husband have decided that our children must "get to know one another better" before they make the final step. My fear is that if they get to know one another too well they won't make it.

8/17/68 My cousin-in-law, Don Mewhiney, a great p***k all his life, has not improved over the years. I am glad he settled in California.

8/19/68 She is over at Dale's spilling her guts. I hope she can't get them back in.

8/13/69 He sat in living room and talked almost a full hour about somebody we did not know doing something we never did figure out. Layna said she got the message but I'll be damned if I did.

8/14/69 To Rainy Lake Lodge for birthday dinner for Jane. The Dr. Edwardses along. We split the check which included drinks by Layna, Jane, Byrne and I. I wonder if they ever paid for liquor before!

12/8/69 Saw Jim's R.L. pictures - good! I clipped Jimmy when no one was watching. Think it did him some good. Sure it did me.

1/17/70 I am amazed that anyone understands what goes on inside one of those boxes [computers], and much more amazed that is should be an offspring of mine.

3/2/70 We have had a great time in Florida but Minnesota calls. Our kids mean much more to us than a little warm weather.

3/24/70 I don't think we helped him a great deal - possibly confused him more, which is generally true in giving or taking advice.

5/9/70 Mildred on cigarette habit to Warren "Why do you spend so much money killing yourself smoking when you can do it just as easy for nothing!"

5/11/70 Bernice starting season on a bitchy note. Already she is hiding the cookies!

6/12/70 Buck started school in 1933 making it 37 years we have had a kid in school. Now four college graduates!

7/30/70 Took Tim and Bradley fishing. Brad never shut up once. He said "Grandfather, do the loons holler to call in the fish so they can catch them? If not, why do they just sit there and blab?" "They are just like you", I told him.

9/6/70 Life is full of worries for most people and ours have had a minimum, according to most standards.

11/20/70 I was down on my knees hacking away (the pipe was barely scratched) when John said "Just about time to holla timba". What a kid!

12/13/70 A big success. About 100 people including Lisa & Jill, who sang and Timmy & Jayme who ate.

12/28/70 I finally proposed that we heat carburetor with blow torch. "Is it absolutely safe?" asked Jim. "Nothing is" I answered.

4/6/71 She has grown up from a lovable kid to a great lady. She was, is and I am sure will be, a parent's joy.

7/1/71 Said Jane "I am on vacation and just don't want to have to think." She learned that want to or not, she had to when she ran out of gas about 300 yards from our island on way home!

9/30/71 As I sat reading the paper, Layna came and put her arms around me and said, "We are very rich to be able to leave a beautiful island and come into this lovely home". I agreed.

12/31/71 Karen rather critical of her parents' weight and said arbitrarily that she would <u>never</u> let herself get that way. A goddamn silly statement in my book.

7/10/72 During the activity, we missed John. All hands out searching. Sally finally found him at north end of island. It reminded Layna and I of other days when we lived at Camp. What mixed emotions come out at a time like that. You don't dare get angry for fear something dreadful has happened. When the lost is found the relief makes anger impossible.

9/17/72 Had a good supper. Prize remark by Layna "What kind of wine <u>are</u> you supposed to serve with wieners?"

5/24/73 Karen wrote a Mother's day letter to Layna (a little late) It was a true classic. She included the old man, too. We agreed that we wouldn't trade one letter like that for both of Moes' Florida condominiums.

8/19/73 As I sit and write, I realize that subconsciously I am feeling sorry for myself. I hate to lose Robin.

1/20/74 I am not a Kissinger so don't know how to bring these opposing forces together.

7/12/74 He says that Brad, Sheila and maybe Tara will be here much of August. I hope we can do them more good than they can do us harm.

Family - 43

8/9/74 A bright spot for her old parents. Jim, while splitting wood, dropped chunk on toe. I felt sorry for him until he took a bad crack at Nixon and I blew up. "He lied!" We agreed on a truce but somehow I got a perverse satisfaction on knowing he had a sore toe.

12/30/74 Layna joined us when we walked the dogs this a.m. Waldo was in his usual high sprits, pulling George around. Said George to Layna "Hold the dog while I tie my shoe lace." Layna answered, "I'll tie the shoe lace."

3/1/75 My first look at grandchild #13. What a honey! Like Ben Haskell said about his sled dog pups, "He has everything ahead of him!"

7/30/75 Little Christopher developing faster than our zucchinis - surely a cute one.

1/1/76 Well, we had 5 great days taking care of Christopher Robin. He is "damned near perfect" - not necessarily a compliment to a mature man but high praise for an 11 month old baby.

2/26/76 I try to tell myself that I owe it to myself (and Buck) to get involved. I am not very convincing.

7/26/76 Sally got me alone and wanted me to speak up as to what was bothering me. Said it would be good for me to get it off my chest. Said I "Sally, I would rather blow a fuse than say one damned word to hurt you because I love you dearly."

4/21/77 I am still clearing brush and making good progress, despite my "help" form Chris. He either is right between my legs or lost so that I have to run after him.

5/13/77 Said I to Layna at bedtime. "Despite frustrations with damned plumbing, this is the spot on earth where I want to be." Says she "Me, too!"

7/24/77 Our Christopher Robin growing out of his sweet little babyhood and developing some damned obnoxious traits.

11/17/77 Buck looked down at Bern's old house and said "Isn't that a cozy little place. It would make a good subject for a Xmas card." We all knew what he meant. The new house is positively ugly.

11/25/77 We baby sat for Chris and Sarah. Sarah an absolute doll, even tho her nose runs much of the time.

1/29/78 The institution of marriage seems to have some backers despite all we read and see on TV.

3/19/78 Home by 7:30. We buried one and we married one. So goes life.

6/25/78 Grandma Nixs confided in me "I can't tell you how happy we all are that Maggie is marrying such a fine boy, with such a fine family!" A good way to end a great day.

7/16/78 When the Prides arrived, Erin jumped out of car and ran toward me on dock "Grandpa, Grandpa, Grandpa" Then - "How's your wife!"

8/11/79 Byrne, Sally and Karen said they still felt the island their home but Buck maintained his home was at Jackfish Bay. He added that he would get together with old folks no matter if it was here, at 265, or Phoenix. When it was over I said, " I think I could have written the script for this gathering."

9/14/79 I arranged with Layna to pick out a Timex watch - me to pay bill. Very sentimental!

10/14/79 We were happy to be able to deliver a healthy dog. I said "Goodbye, little faker". He wagged his tail. I think he knew what I meant.

10/21/79 Said I "I came to tell you that I feel like a s**t for not offering to help yesterday." Buck answered "Don't feel that way, Dad, I enjoy working alone!"

11/20/79 The parents not too perturbed (outwardly), so why should we be? We kept calm (outwardly).

12/9/79 She still is a straw in the wind, not knowing what she wants to do. Well, who does in these turbulent times?

5/11/80 I had Instamatic camera in my jacket pocket and took several pictures of people in water. Some razzing about my cold heart to take pictures instead of jumping into creek to rescue Sarah.

8/17/80 I think Gene has a short fuse where kids are concerned. I have a short fuse where Jean E. is concerned.

9/6/80 There were a few confrontations - kids vs. kids, kids vs. grandparents, grandparents vs. grandparent - none of which lasted very long and none left any permanent scars.

11/8/80 Little Bobby an unusual kid. Stubborn is the old fashioned word for it but there must be a modern term to describe him.

6/24/81 The kids acting their age- whatever that means.

9/3/81 Chris watched TV for two hours and made a terrific fuss when I said I wanted to see news. I watched the news.

9/10/81 Etta carried on the old family tradition of making big plans with not a chance of carrying them out.

9/12/81 Good God, what a rowdy gang. When they say child abuse they must mean abuse from kids to parents.

10/22/81 She came home very pleased with herself. She had ducked the presidency again.

10/27/81 The 3 kids the worst ever. God almighty but I find it difficult to hold my temper. I believe that "parent abuse" is more prevalent than "child abuse."

11/13/81 Layna had to prompt her several times before she said she liked our new furniture.

12/19/81 Shortly after Bobby fell off a stool and banged his head on coffee table. I haven't seen that much blood since I gutted my last deer.

2/13/82 Of our 16 grandchildren, Jayme and Maggie are the best adjusted. I'm glad I gave him my favorite 20 gauge shotgun.

4/18/82 He can still laugh, but it must take considerable effort.

5/5/82 They were all set to go home at 8:00 p.m. when Chris' favorite program came on. The world is on its way to a nuclear war but we could not watch the news. Maybe it is just as well.

7/2/82 Each day Bobby demonstrates the fact that he is more clever than the other NWI inhabitants. He loses a few skirmishes but the battles are his.

8/31/82 Tara and friend Karen left. If the future of our country falls to their kind, we have little to fear.

9/30/82 Layna busy most of day. I was busy getting out of her way.

11/11/82 Bobby loves the word DON'T and is constantly on the move looking for things he shouldn't be doing.

1/22/83 To make sure we knew that she was a woman's libber, Sarah got Bobby down on floor and pounded him with her fists. Grandma threw her out.

2/14/83 We didn't make any arrangements but he said I could stay with them. Sally called and invited me to their home. There is hay in the manger for this old babe.

6/20/83 Robin brought the cats, Hans Schumacher brought Duncan. We are the home for unwanted pets.

8/4/83 Karen and kids off for Cass Lake where they will attend Unitarian summer family camp. Karen a little concerned as to how it will work out. She has a reason to be. Hard telling what her 3 kids will do to the organization.

8/9/83 He (Ted) told me later "Your two boys have surely inherited your story telling ability." I am not sure that that is an asset.

9/4/83 She is so calm outwardly but I know she is churning inwardly. Well, she is a professional counselor. Hope she gives herself good advice.

10/13/83 Robin desperate for a baby sitter. He called Layna who was going to RLWC meeting. I volunteered, much to amazement of all concerned (me too).

3/10/84 I feel like shaking hell out of him but realize it might help me but could raise Cain with family harmony.

6/27/84 Karen's last day on island and I have been on verge of tears all day. Many things left unsaid and undone, altho I feel closer to her now than in many years. A remarkable woman. May fate be good to her and her little brood.

7/9/84 Byrne and Jim F. moved mail box. Layna ran by driveway because she had lost her landmark.

8/15/84 When Layna asked Buck to comment on the strained relationship between Ted and Gene, he said, "I don't pay any attention to anything that doesn't pertain to Curtice Island!"

9/14/84 Jim and I alone at 265 for couple of hours. Much to talk about. He told me what I have known for years, that he is, and always has been, amazed at the Johnson generosity. I told him about our experience with the Pennsylvania Dutch in 1929. I hope he got the message.

10/6/84 When we were all commenting on the fine meal Sarah said "It was a lot better than I ever expected!"

10/19/84 Layna home at 6:30 and I hadn't done one damned thing about making supper. What a helpless old fart! She says she loves me. I wonder why.

11/3/84 They are fairly well behaved as long as she keeps yelling at them.

12/22/84 Buck came for coffee and gave us a blow by blow of the last days of Bern Minter's moving. He was in on most of it and came out with a great admiration for that old lady. I always did have a goodly amount of it but it was hidden by her faults. That can be said about most of us.

1/13/85 The 3 kids romped in the snow like a family of otters.

2/23/85 Layna cut Bobby's and Chris' hair. Bob hollered so loud that I feared a call from the sheriff on a child abuse charge.

2/24/85 He told about taking a sauna then jumping in ice hole on lake. He said that the handicapped people didn't do it. Who is handicapped?

5/27/85 There was but little agreement when I said it is mostly a case of plain luck if kids turn out all right!

6/22/85 The 2½ year old kid fits right in to the galaxy of stars of our offspring.

5/9/86 As he left, I had an overwhelming impulse to give him a big hug but a car drove into the yard and the spell was broken.

Chapter 7 – Friends

- *Throughout the years on Rainy Lake, the Johnsons had a number of friends who would drop in, or be dropped in on, for coffee or a drink or a game of cards.*

3/19/45 Would have tried the car but Lou made a few sarcastic remarks that made me think the walk would do her good.

5/9/50 They are among our best friends, but, by God, they sure are just camping out!

1/12/51 Seems like Cliff and Lou can discuss people without getting malicious better than anyone we know.

2/17/53 Finally saw Lou Moe's new hair do - the most controversial subject to hit Ranier since the municipal liquor store deal.

9/3/53 They have one of the most modern homes in America in Downers Grove and live as primitive as the Indians up here.

10/3/57 Car found and Judy mad at Indians because they knew and wouldn't tell. I look at it differently, all the poor bastards have left is their loyalty to one another.

7/20/64 Norman and Vi here in evening. They are all shook up about REA pole spoiling their view. Everyone wants a million acres - and the hell with anyone else.

7/3/61 Only bright spot in day when Lou Moe dropped in to enumerate her troubles. The more she talked, the better I felt.

8/16/65 I was full of great stories concerning my adventures with the top brass of B.C., but Harry anxious to tell me of his 2 hour fishing expedition with the Lear Jet pilots. I let him go, and said nothing. There are few good listeners left in this world.

4/20/66 He is lonesome, which must be as bad as any ailment known to man.

12/27/66 Now the "Pearson Philosophers" will get the news and much will come out of it - all worthless.

12/28/66 I will never learn how the fishing was. For 35 years I have known Cliff to soak up every bit of information available while giving not an iota in return. Some of the stuff he got out of me the past few years hasn't been exactly reliable - and I get a perverse enjoyment out of dishing it out.

1/1/67 Harry Davey, in discussing the Nims said, "They will come for a meal at the drop of a hint."

1/16/67 The rumor mongers were at their vicious best today.

1/23/67 Mr. & Mrs. D. Johnson are not beyond criticism in talking about their friends. We tell ourselves it is O.K. just so we don't discuss this with anyone else - which we don't.

3/10/67 The part about Jim drew considerable comment via telephone. Judy said he could see the tears thru the ink. Well, he should, they were there.

4/17/68 Cliff Moe in hospital to get hemorrhoids removed. Lou out for dinner. She described his operation vividly enough so that my rear end is sore.

2/18/70 They make a great show of being completely happy but I think we would need more to do than play golf some of the time and talk about it the rest.

2/24/70 When we were walking, George commented on how poor Ardys was at giving directions while they were driving. Said he "She can teach second graders how to do modern math but if she were to tell you how to pick up that shell, you would strain your back!"

12/3/70 Can't understand why Harry is looking beyond that gal. Maybe she is unattainable.

1/31/71 I finally learned what makes George George. He lives with two maiden sisters.

5/3/71 It must be vedy, vedy plush. Hard for us to visualize Cliff in that environment.

5/7/71 Harry out for supper. He gets married tomorrow to end an 18 month period of celibacy. He hated every minute of it.

6/27/71 No great argument put on by Les & Marie but a good time nevertheless.

8/19/71 I think Opal is really working up some sympathy for this remarkable man with all the handicaps who is trying to lead a normal life.

10/22/71 I can thank the Red Gods that the blood in my eyes doesn't prevent me from seeing the spectacular beauty around me as is does for Opal. Poor Wayne, he can't see at all.

12/7/71 One address book was at least 15 years old. Many names of people who are not in reach of anyone on this earth.

3/24/72 Dan worse that a fart in a mitten this a.m. He woke up at 4 a.m. thinking he should go to Minnesota <u>today</u> to buy cattle.

5/31/72 Cliff's hearing much worse, but he doesn't thrive on small talk so I don't think it bothers him too much.

7/24/72 We definitely have had - and will have - altogether too many people at island this summer. I would hate to eliminate these two.

1/13/73 He's not getting any more information out of me until a teensy weensie bit is returned.

7/14/73 Did not tell them about my fishing - following an old policy of letting no valuable information leak to Cliff.

6/8/74 Marie and Les in fine form. They are like a couple of prize fighters who are in prime condition to battle one another. No blood shed, however.

8/24/74 People, people, people. Well, it's not that bad. Maybe, down deep, I have much affection for the human race. I know Layna has.

2/3/75 I grabbed the little bugger and gave him a great hug and squeeze. I then choked up so I couldn't talk. Neither could he and off he went. It took some time before I regained my composure.

7/27/75 They surely must be our very favorite people - and we have some dandies

10/20/75 We had a long talk - Cliff told me about Leonard Peterson giving him a bad deal in the division of game - also very critical of people who wouldn't give away something that they had no use for!! My God, are we all that blind to our own faults?

1/13/76 She is less opinionated as she gets older and we enjoy her company. Maybe we are getting more tolerant.

3/27/76 I decided to write an article for the "Chronicle" about Spike. It went pretty good after I wrote "I want to share some of the memories of a friendship I had with a man for over 40 years, a man true to himself, who would do anything for you if he liked you and anything to you if he didn't".

12/25/76 We invited the Moes, as we have in the past, to have Xmas dinner with us. They came, each bearing a ½ gal. jug of wine. At a 7 course dinner, enjoyed by all, we almost killed one of the bottles. When our friends prepared to leave, Layna said "We didn't open one of the wine bottles, why don't you take it with you?" and I'll be goddamned if the didn't carry it away! Now that I have written it, I say to myself "Who is chicken s**t in this deal, the Moes for their behavior or me for writing it down?" Probably both.

7/3/77 Les still having difficulty understanding that Marie is 87 years old. She treats him like a 14 year old so it balances out.

7/20/77 Said Les, "If I could run through this life again, I would like to start out as a Johnson." His voice full of emotion as he said it. High praise!

11/1/77 I thot Cliff rather philosophical but realized no one could figure out what was going thru that Norwegian's head.

2/1/78 Someone had told him that the horseshoe over the basement stairs were upside down. The good luck could run out, which explained why both he and Opal had fallen down the steps. I reversed it and he feels luckier - I told him he should still hang onto the railing.

6/17/78 When Layna asked him yesterday if he had any commitments for today he said "If I had, I would cancel them to be with your gang!"

6/27/78 Layna and I agreed that they join forces to make the greatest bulls**tting team of all time. Fun tho!

10/23/78 Also talked to Lardy who said that Sharon had told him we were dearer to her than her own folks!

1/2/79 As he left we learned that he was avoiding female company at his house. We were glad to provide a refuge.

8/1/79 I caught up with him as he left dock. He came back and I grabbed his hand and said, "I can't let you go without telling you that you were a helluva good neighbor". He said "You were the good neighbors!"

1/25/80 At 5:00 p.m. George and Maria came after us (raining hard) and we went to their $200,000 home where we huddled around the fireplace in their bedroom, drinking brandy, for a couple of hours.

5/2/80 I have written many letters of that type in past years so have a pretty good idea what she had to do.

7/15/82 Lou has become less talkative as the years go by, not nearly as positive in her statements. Very becoming.

3/4/83 George takes good care of his equipment but doesn't baby it when a logging road beckons.

9/28/83 They were full of talk about their new summer home on Swell Bay. Cliff's all in favor of the proposed restrictions. He wants all of Swell Bay for himself.

9/30/83 She was very bitter concerning Pete Peterson's relationship with Carl. I am bitter about Grace's relationship with Carl.

3/18/85 Layna asked Jim, "When is the lake going to open up?" Jim said "May 3". Layna "That is a good guess." Jim "That is <u>not</u> a guess!" Smart Indian.

8/10/85 Ted in a class by himself, far out snoring Carl Harrison, Ed LaFave and Layna.

12/30/85 She told about taking care of her sister's kids for a couple of days and said "That satisfied my mother's instinct for another year."

10/7/86 He reminds me of the old Indians who understood only when it suited them.

Chapter 8 - Neighbors

- *I am grouping as neighbors all of the friends and acquaintances just outside of the circle that I am calling friends.*

1/11/40 Could only stay a minute so wouldn't take off coats. Left at 11:30. Didn't have to put on coats as they were still on.

1/9/45 Classic remark by Mary, "You're sure that cake is good if Pepper (the dog) eats it. He don't eat nothin' if it ain't good!"

2/19/45 Seriously thought of bouncing something off his head but he stopped just in time.

8/3/45 Fitzgerald outfit a little screwy - don't know if I like them or not.

4/2/46 Arnold and Mabes over in evening for a while. Much general gossip - but no one told anyone anything!

2/5/47 Stopped at Wagness'. Heard all about Ernie deal. Also overjoyed at hearing ice job cost Major <u>$70.00</u>! Not such a bad world after all

2/16/47 Byrne went along to help pull toboggan and kids as Burt and Hugh had hard time coming over! I guess we are a tough family - maybe only by comparison with the city softies.

3/5/48 Mabes and Arnold came over in evening - much talk but nothing to the point - any point.

8/18/48 Stopped at Major Roberts and the hypocritical bastard hid rather than serve drinks to such a mob!

8/20/48 Stopped in at Scheldrup's where the old boy got a $150 consultation for $.40 worth of wine!

7/14/49 Passed Major Roberts boat at anchor and gave him the works. I'll bet he was so goddamn mad he couldn't swear.

2/4/50 Have known the Olsons for 20 years and it has ever been the same. It can't be possible that they hear only exaggerated versions of all doings. The exaggeration must be theirs!

2/6/50 If she were mine, I would try at least one good kick at her rear end in the hopes it might jar something loose that even an x-ray can't detect. It wouldn't do much harm, and sure to hell would make me feel better!

2/11/50 Ernie and Gertie to and from island by snow shoes. Tough deal when you have $1600 invested in a tractor and have to walk.

2/12/50 Many people threatened to walk out, but no one came. People we know are a bunch of sissies.

1/30/50 Said Harry "It was your own damned fault that you couldn't start your car - anybody who has monkeyed around with machinery as long as you should have bought a Ford in the first place. It says right on the radio that there are more Fords sold in Canada than any other kind."

5/5/50 He needs a good hate like other people need a tonic!

5/16/50 As I have thot for many years, the only one more unreasonable than that type of fellow is one who argues with him!

11/15/50 Paul's comment on buildings on [Ober's] island, "This architecture not the result of a normal mind!"

1/10/51 Lawrence and I in argument over high water, which as usual in such cases, got us nowhere.

1/22/51 Layna, along with Rainy Lake Women's Club delegation to Ranier where they opposed proposal of Village Council to put liquor store in community building. It must have been a real knock down and drag out affair, and I, for one, would just as soon get it second hand. Goddamn such a bunch of idiots. Ranier has finest town site in northern Minnesota, but due to their infernal wrangling, it is still a primitive town - with primitive people, for the most part!

1/26/51 Stopped at Finstad's and got low down on liquor store move from Clara. She is on a crusade and glows under it. I am full of apathy in a case like this and don't know if I am proud of it or not. Maybe my indifference is because I "can't be bothered."

2/7/51 Olsons bought a new Kaiser about 2 weeks ago, $2,900. That has given long noses, including ourselves, plenty to talk about. They have had some trouble with it, and due to the perversity of human nature, no one is sorry for them.

2/12/51 Looks like I haven't much on my mind when I write so much about other people. Our own lives are so happy that anything different in our friends is worthy of comment.

8/2/51 Ready to eat when Major Roberts came into bay. Exchanged visits and the old bastard is as full of B.S. as ever. My stomach can't take too much of that stuff - and I'm tough.

8/31/51 A fine time spoiled for me by that "Stinky" Dr. Kinports. He inferred that old Fitzgerald had been tight when he broke his leg. I thot I had built up a resistance against all heels, but found out that I can still be hurt..

1/24/52 Karen says Harrisons have a "grouchy" house! "From the mouth of babes".

1/15/53 To McKenna's for a real gab fest. Just sat and panned our friends. Olive got 89% of the words which should make her happy. The Olsons for a good share of what was left.

3/4/52 She told Layna a few years ago that you could do anything if you had money, but now she isn't so sure.

3/12/52 I sure never could have lived the life I have with a woman like that.

4/8/52 A case where from all outside appearances, people are 100% set for life - good home, job, family and all that goes with it, but still dissatisfied.

4/15/52 Gerald & I had fun ribbing Olive over Lee Boy learning facts of life from baby sitter. He is now seven and we both said we regretted lost time (due to ignorance) in our own lives. I said I felt keenly loss of sex life from 7 - 12 and Olive almost ran me out of house.

4/30/52 Ernie pretty drunk - and spouting off at the mouth on many subjects.

1/5/53 Biggest news item from her: "Lee Boy now knows there is no Santa Claus and is much relieved!" He is 9. Karen was that smart at 3 - or 2!

2/28/53 Florence definitely showing the effects of the barrels of alcohol she has consumed in her 40 years.

3/18/53 If I had invited anyone as often in the past 2 years and got turned down, I would have let them go to hell.

7/25/53 found Major Roberts there. Bull s**t knee deep before we left - some of it mine.

1/27/54 He has reached the point where he would use violence, if he only knew where to direct it.

8/11/54 He is one of the few people I know who has a helluva lot more on the ball than he advertises.

10/13/54 Louie had been drinking and talking foolish. He was due!

11/1/54 Lawrence intercepted a card from her mother. In effect it said "You are doomed, dear, Goodbye!"

12/4/54 Ober told about almost breaking in [falling through the ice] yesterday. It will ever be the same - the mail <u>must</u> go thru, even tho it means his life. Hooey!

12/26/54 I don't think she loves the great outdoors quite as much when there is that much effort & discomfort connected with it.

3/16/55 It seems that $10,000 at this time might put them right in the swim, socially (up to now a tough job) besides assuring some real consideration on judgment day. Poor little Dick and Joan, belonging to the same church, are about to give it up as being too expensive. I think God will understand - in all cases!

2/25/56 To Laitalas for pre-dance drinks. Houskas, Manillas, Makinens. The names made me feel I was back in school at Buck Lake.

12/1/56 If Jim's insurance adjuster could have been on that trip, Jim would never collect a damned cent from his accident. He sure is far from disabled!

1/11/57 I would sure hate to carry him off to the cemetery now that he has found the best happiness in years.

2/21/57 He is getting along a lot better than I thot he would and a lot poorer than he thot he would.

6/16/58 On the other hand, we haven't been spiteful with anyone up till now, which is poor training in dealing with a p***k.

4/19/59 Carl here at noon. Poor bastard, almost ecstatic over fact that Grace had called and was in a good mood. Their relationship reminds me of me and Klinker. I could put her in the dumps with a cross word.

4/28/59 "He is doing what he can to clear up a mess, but by God, there was no mess until he got up on Rainy Lake!"

12/10/59 It will go down in the memories of all of us as the "I" speech. He used the word 6 times in each sentence, and there were many sentences.

3/18/60 I can't make myself sorry for the mean things I have said about him.

3/19/60 He closed with his itinerary for the next 6 months so they will be sure and not miss a payment! The old bastard!

3/22/60 Karen and I to McKenna's for dinner - Ruth, a horrible cook, outdid herself on this one. Even the toast was burned.

4/3/60 I commented that it would have been a shame to go a whole winter without digging a car out at least once but my remark was not well received.

4/24/60 It seems to me that her skin should be thicker after dealing with square dancers all these years.

5/1/60 I gave Jerry "the ground is always frozen for lazy hogs" routine, and he kept going.

5/25/60 It was a bad show, I hope I never feel important enough to talk to any fellow mortal like that.

7/20/60 I gave my appraisal of Maj. Roberts and Walter said I should have been a psychiatrist. He should hear me when I really warm up on that subject.

1/20/61 I left for home happy to have thot of something that would sic them on one another rather than on me. Got home to think of many clever things I could have said. Maybe just as well that I didn't.

1/24/61 It is hard to get 3 or more people to agree on anything.

4/15/61 There is no question about Wally - a true nobleman, altho gone astray at times.

7/28/61 They are smart people - they think like me!

8/14/61 [Dr. Scheldrup] He can't last many more years - and I am afraid not long enough for me to learn to like him.

8/14/61 [Dr. Scheldrup] That is one of the things I don't like about him. This book too small to list all of them.

9/21/61 Talbert offered to pay and I charged our usual fee, the one established in 1929 - nothing!

12/11/61 Gerald stopped for 2 drinks and a million word conversation.

3/4/62 I took a tape recording of their activities. Sounded like 200 seagulls around a commercial fisherman lifting his net..

3/24/62 I had hopes of seeing some deer. We did - 7 of them. No doubt there would have been more but Jim's voice scared even the ravens.

1/7/63 Clara took the opportunity to tell me how she was advising so and so about such and such. She paid me a great compliment by not offering any free advice to me.

4/17/63 I am sure that if science had perfected an "enthusiasm meter" we would have blown a fuse out of it.

3/4/64 Our neighborliness has sure gone to hell when we can't see old friends more often than we do.

11/23/64 He is a garrulous old bugger and talked constantly about moose, bees, and violin making. I was too sleepy to appreciate any of it.

12/25/64 Gerald stopped for couple of drinks and left many bushels of bull.

12/31/64 To Alan Tibbits home in Fort with Daveys for cocktails along with about 20 others, we knew none when we went and knew none when we got home. They did not fraternize.

1/28/65 I am not going to say "I told you so", so help me God, but it will be difficult to keep quiet.

2/16/65 I get my information from the high and low and repeat it to no one.

2/24/65 I criticize myself at times because I lack an opinion - but this is worse.

4/29/65 They have "gone steady' for more that 20 years. If they get married, it won't be a shotgun deal.

5/10/65 I told Layna I was glad Artie drank. When she asked why, I said "he would be absolutely perfect if he didn't!"

4/10/66 It is at Easter that I think of Fern Laurion's remark made years ago. "I like to go to Catholic church on Christmas and Easter. That's when you can see all the whores, pimps and taxicab drivers!"

2/2/67 Maybe I summed up my feelings when I told Layna "If an old dog was tied up down there I would feel obligated to go down and feed him every day - and would expect as much thanks or pay!"

4/15/67 Saw Bill Eddy at Rest Home. Said he "I am 85 years old, and I never had it so good!"

8/8/67 No thot of marrying the gal, however. Well, they have been "going together" for about 25 years so haven't had time to make up their minds.

8/23/67 I am sure we all remember well what we said but a bit fuzzy about anything anyone else said. No wonder "lack of communication" has become a byword.

9/23/67 In retrospect, I know it was much better before John Barleycorn joined the chorus.

12/11/67 Hope he got good reception on his new colored TV It was so great in black and white that I don't know if we could stand the color.

2/22/68 Did not seem very sad when we told him about Jim DiOnne's passing. He must have heard that Jim said he was a pee poor gunsmith.

4/23/68 She came home with a present from Mary. It was an 8 X 10 picture of Emil in his coffin! It went up the chimney.

7/27/68 Dan an impatient man. Must be a bugger to live with. I wouldn't want to try living with Eileen either, for that matter.

10/31/68 Surely I was never closer to any man in my lifetime - and that goes for my father and Buck.

12/15/68 Anyone as old as I am must have reason at times to say "I should have" or "I could have" but certainly we never messed our lives up like those people.

12/23/68 She chattered constantly until I gave up and to bed at 11:00. I wonder who listens when she is with her mother.

1/7/69 She is not my favorite acquaintance. She gave us a complete run down on her "flu". She certainly did not hear a word Layna said. She didn't hear me either. I didn't say anything.

8/9/69 Stopped at Boyd's for ½ hour. He still thinks that he pays more taxes than anyone. Hard to explain things to some people.

11/21/69 I told him that Grace had given 25 years of her life making a man out of him and he would not be true to her memory if he let her down now. Fine words, Johnson, how would you take a blow like this?

11/27/69 In the "olden days" we used to feed the old lake bachelors, now we have the widows.

12/17/69 One of my molars needing filling so I went to see Dr. Milroy. He is getting senile! He talked on and on. A typical garrulous old man of 80. He is 65.

1/10/70 There are literally hundreds of jigs and spoons of all sizes. He [Jim DiOnne] must have spent a great deal of time on this, but it must have been during the period when he was mad at me because I knew little of this activity.

1/11/70 She still thinks she married beneath her. What a firm foundation to build an unhappy marriage..

3/15/70 The conversation went thusly: 80% Margaret, 19% Lou, Layna, Don, Gene 1%. When they got up to leave at 9 p.m. Margaret said "It is great to get into a stimulating discussion once in a while!"

9/1/70 We agreed they were a great family. The kind the newspapers overlook in favor of the hippies.

9/12/70 Brian said he had 57 boxes of rifle and pistol shells loaded. Said Willie, "Good thing you weren't born 100 years ago, there wouldn't have been an Indian left." "Ya", put in Jim, "We wouldn't even be here!"

12/7/70 "Yak, yak, yak. I'll get even, blah, blah, blah." If she was mine, I'd drown her.

12/22/70 For years I have suspected Gene of exaggerating a little and tonight I confirmed these suspicions. This is not a criticism, just a comment.

1/14/71 After lunch I took off on snowmobile and ran back thru big swamp. Met Jim DiOnne in a dozen places. I wonder how he would have felt about the snowmobile. Probably would have started shooting by now.

1/16/71 She is a #1 boor in any group, including one in her own home.

1/26/71 Three Manhattans and we got engaged in some brilliant conversation. Much about ecology, which none of us knew much about.

3/20/71 I keep telling him I know very little about it. In my own mind, I realize the futility of it all. Even if I did know the answer he would pay no attention.

6/23/71 A great cocktail hour, joined by the Switzers and Foxes who stayed too long. Our charcoal fire almost went out waiting for them to leave.

1/3/72 A highly intelligent, and opinionated man. I enjoy his conversation.

1/31/72 Got tied up an hour listening to Clara's blah, blah. It was particularly irritating when I wanted to listen to George, who is always interesting to me.

5/2/72 A great pair, as opposite as two men can be but obviously fond of one another.

6/23/72 Now she has decided to become an MD which means another 4 years in school. I don't think we could afford her for a daughter.

7/24/72 I guess he is like the most of us, a great guy when everything goes his way - but don't cross me!

7/26/72 I will bet NWI against Garbage Island that he won't buy a boat this summer!

10/20/72 A great example of one whose ambitions exceeded his capabilities.

1/7/73 My God, what a talking pair. They asked us to come because they are planning a trip. They didn't hear a damned one of the few works uttered by us.

3/13/73 I tried to show my displeasure by not asking him to sit down. I am getting intolerant and it's not fun.

3/18/73 They talked constantly and now I can't remember a damned thing except that I am sure irritated as all hell. Lord, keep me from becoming a bore like that.

4/9/73 I can understand Spanish better than the English spoken by the Oien boys. I <u>think</u> we reserved dock space for Clark's boat.

4/16/73 Dale had folder from "Musket Inn". Very verbose - and full of bull s**t, too.

11/29/73 The Porters moved out without saying "goodbye". Not strange, they hardly said "hello" the year and a half that they were there.

2/6/74 To Oberholtzer's birthday party (90th) at rest home. About 30 friends sat and drank coffee, ate cake and wondered what kept him alive all these years.

2/10/74 He stayed to watch 3 hour show *Good, Bad and Ugly*. We enjoyed his company more than the picture, which was pretty damned good.

8/4/74 The usual high class bulls**t from both of them. Layna said when they left, "Gerald stopped in to see if the stories he has been telling about your health are true!"

9/26/74 Little Heidi put on quite a show, even went to potty. What a fuss we make over our natural functions!

10/17/74 As I have known for years, and had no reason to change my opinion, he is a high class bulls**tter.

8/23/75 Rudy a pompous ass in many ways and the fact that he has made so much money makes him think he is a great conversationalist.

10/22/75 Francis one of the better narrators of all time. (His wife, Joyce, said "bulls**tter", but if that is what it is, it is a very high class brand).

11/24/75 Like most people after advice, he wanted us to agree with his already made decision.

3/7/76 A yak, yak battle between Eileen and Margaret. Margaret gave up early, she must have felt outclassed.

3/21/76 I have no new ideas of any consequence and tell myself that none is better than one as impractical as the one she proposed.

6/8/76 Got into a rather lively discussion concerning Ober's Island. No one converted anyone else altho Layna made it clear that all this "shrine" talk was a lot of bull.

8/20/77 Seldom do I get the opportunity of giving so much with so little effort on my part. He seemed very grateful.

9/20/77 Was all set to go fishing in evening when Marvin Kruskopf came. He chewed rag until it was almost dark. Wasn't a very good evening anyhow!

12/8/77 Then went on to say that had he stayed in Navy he would now be retired with a Captains pension <u>BUT</u>, like most retired navy personnel would be a drunk. He was actually staggering as he said it!

12/31/77 A bitter, cynical man with deep contempt for much of human race but mostly for lawyers and ministers. "Lawyers are so crooked they have to screw their sox on". "The intelligence of most ministers equals a mosquito's fart". Of his fellow man he says (among many other disparaging observations) "Man is proud of his sexual prowess which is equaled by any dog and exceeded greatly by any jackass".

8/8/78 While at Musket Inn, Peggy told us that Shawn, aged <u>8</u>, had run 140 hp kicker to Tilson Creek to pick up guests! Unbelievable! Am I a fuddy-duddy or is this unacceptable behavior?

8/10/78 As I cleaned fish, young Greg (8 years old) bombarded me with questions. Said I "How come you ask so many questions?" Said he "Because I'm so dumb!" "Far from it", I thot.

1/27/79 As Swede Charlie is supposed to have said, "Those three gals make a fine pair."

9/3/79 Pat on way home. I can live well without that smart ass.

9/17/79 As Carlson would have said, "It was the worst wonderful thing I ever saw."

9/28/79 I wish I could tell if he is awfully smart or awfully full of bulls**t. More than likely, he is both.

11/19/79 Ted Hall's *Chronicle* carried an obituary of Gilda Dahlberg. It was a masterpiece. Pictures furnished by Don & Layna. He concluded by saying that the tears shed by the natives on hearing of her demise did not appreciably raise the level of Rainy Lake. How true!

11/29/79 He is a real bulls**tter but not obnoxious on a short visit. Rather enjoyed it.

12/1/79 Tommy caught the hunting bug last fall and likes to come over and swap yarns. I can imagine him talking when he gets older and I am gone, saying "When I was a kid we lived next door to an old man - - - - - ."

7/1/80 He [Ted Hall] indicated that he had recently grown out of the notion that Oberholtzer was God.

12/16/80 We have known her for 51 years. Our relationship clouded by the presence of that arrogant little bastard, Gilbert

3/24/81 Jim Froehlich here to show off his latest toy. A Honda 3-wheeler. There is a lot of boy wrapped up in that big frame.

7/14/81 I would like to have heard their conversation- or maybe I wouldn't.

12/4/81 Like Cinderella, when the clock struck 9:00 p.m., they headed for home. Their dog's bladder only good for 4 hours. We have made our share of mistakes over a period of years but escaped being tied down by a pet.

2/17/82 He is a good talker and a great listener. He should be after living with Margaret so many years.

3/8/82 We have known them since Kooch-i-ching days and thought he was deaf & dumb. Today I drew him out and learned he was neither. I enjoyed his company.

3/18/82 Said Al "I don't give a damn if I can't remember somebody from 40 years ago. The hell with them. I am living for today and tomorrow."

7/30/82 The house designed by Cowgill. I have decided that a good design by him has one qualification. Wherever one board will do the job, be sure that you use 3 or 4 or maybe a dozen.

9/24/83 Arden Erickson almost wet her pants when I said "This boat reminds me of the *Ethel B*".

10/4/83 Full of talk, most of it interesting. However, he is a poor listener.

11/2/83 He was a cantankerous old bastard. His dogs reflected his temperament - they were <u>mean!</u>

1/1/84 Fine people of a different set of values from ours. Music, art, literature - in a way I envy them but somehow we have struggled along without it.

2/18/84 At Dick Ellingson's party he gave special thanks to different ones there. He said of Francis Einarson, "I owe him a debt of gratitude. If it wasn't for him we would not have had our baby daughter!" The place exploded.

2/20/84 How can a person as smart as she is do something that dumb.

3/8/84 She talked non stop for 1½ hours. Hardly a word from rest of us. To make matters worse, I knew that Hibbing was playing Edina in the state hockey tournament. When they left, I laid down on my bed and cried.

3/23/84 Republic Airlines in deep financial trouble. Some talk about moving out of the Falls. Don't know what we would do if they pulled out, taking our neighbors with them.

3/27/84 When she was asked to say grace, she mumbled a few words that even the Lord would have trouble understanding.

11/11/84 Clara Finstad there talking almost constantly. A forlorn little woman who still feels the loss of her partner, George.

11/22/84 Said Clara, "Are there any of the old timers living around here any more?" and Layna said "Clara, we are the old timers."

2/10/86 A know it all, ever ready to share his vast store among a captive audience. I won't miss him.

8/31/86 Some heady conversation. Three strong women's libbers and it appears that they are planning an eventual takeover. They named women who were captains of industry, leaders in education, medicine, politics, on and on. After listening to them, I thot "Why not?" They can't screw it all up worse than it is under male leadership.

Chapter 9 - Work

- *The quotes in this section are really a mixed bag but seem to have some connection to productive labor.*

10/7/42 Picked cranberries. Layna and I got 42 pounds and 2 sore backs.

2/6/45 Layna made donuts and apple pies and we spent all afternoon trying to eat them up. The hell of it is that I can't enjoy loafing when there is so much to do.

2/23/45 One of those days when everything ass backwards. Small saw is still hung in birch where I threw it!

3/1/45 Ernie world's champion screwer upper. Never happier than when he is twisting on a valve or nut that he doesn't understand - just in case it might help. When we finally got so tired that we couldn't turn over that chunk of pig iron anymore with the crank, we gave up.

7/11/45 Seems like the work goes slower as it goes along. If all carpenters work that way, the building trades are due for a revolution. No common man can afford to pay for that kind of stuff.

10/11/45 Helen made cookies with the same amount of fuss that Layna makes in preparing a dinner for 20.

12/18/45 Finished ceiling in bedroom. It was quite a job - like many others - nothing to actually putting up the things that count, in this case the Insulite, but a lot of monkey business getting things lined up.

12/29/45 Andersons, Albert, Oscar, Ernie, stopped in about 3 p.m. "We would stay awhile and visit if you weren't so busy!" Goddamn. They couldn't stay and help?

1/31/46 After supper went at letters again and finished up at 10. Funny the stamps didn't curl off some of those! I guess mine weren't much better.

3/25/46 Harry cut as fast as Byrne and I could haul - that isn't to tell how fast he was but rather how slow we were.

4/25/46 Had plenty of advice from Fulsam,. Murray, Steele and a few others and contrary to the general thing, most of it was good.

3/27/47 Got into a real discussion (not argument) on cutting rafters. Finally got a 2 x 4 solid full of marks but when we made the cut, it was the right one.

4/13/47 Finally hit a snag on the ice business as anybody with an ounce of brains knew we would. You just can't go on having things your own way when dealing with that stuff.

5/4/47 Got into long winded discussion with boys over dock. Very interesting but tiring.

12/1/47 First day back to work and nothing doing. Listened to Retter go on and on which was work enough in itself.

3/29/48 Paid Dick Haney $48 for 6 days work. This should make interesting reading when we hit another depression.

5/13/48 Have plenty of reason to worry about my decision to put boat in Swell Bay. Seems like I am only one who likes it here. To hell with them. I'll make them like it!

4/3/49 Back in the ice business again! The damned work must be in my blood, because every year I curse it and swear I'll never get sucked in again and - here I am!

6/2/49 Gassed up our cruiser, put in battery but couldn't start engine. Time raced along, I got nervous but that didn't put spark to plugs.

1/26/50 Harry Robinson has new interest in life now that he is official plugger inner for car heater.

2/20/50 A helluva tough job which went further to substantiate what I have known for years - the best way to cross two miles of lake is on snowshoes.

4/2/50 Not many arguments as to procedure. Must be a simple job for that to happen.

6/8/50 Sam, the Kooch-i-ching watchman "watches" as valuable equipment goes under.

9/22/50 I never cared much for the people but it does bring a lump to my throat when I think of what those places were when Frank & Audrey and Don & Layna were the slaves that kept them up - with no appreciation from the masters

11/13/50 The "Miracle" as I see it is how in hell he [Ober] ever got by all these years. The most unpractical man alive. Says he " you fellows do things with so much ease" Thot I, "It sure is easy for you when we do it."

3/15/51 Two pails at a time, and after each trip the hole moved out 100 yards and house slid up hill another 40 feet.

2/13/52 I was tolerant of that bitch as long as she left me alone, and the same goes for this son of a bitch.

5/2/52 There is considerable confusion on that job - and as in all big corporations, as far as I can see, the most important thing for each individual is to not stick his neck out far enough to get it cut off!

7/25/52 It is a job that just can't be done alone (not by me, at least) and I crawled in and out of it 40 times a day trying to be two places at the same time. A ten year old boy could have saved me hours.

9/11/52 I fried fish as I had seen Layna & Sally do (never before in my life) and got the usual raves.

10/3/52 I was dead tired when we got in so by the same token, he should have been dead!

1/20/53 God but those power tools are strange implements in my hands. Hope I'm not too old to get used to them.

6/3/53 I mildly considered giving up but as long as Buck didn't mention it, I kept on.

8/12/53 Many, many, friends(?) stop to chew fat and offer advice but not a damned one offered to cut or pick up a twig. This is not a complaint - merely an observation.

12/7/53 Gave goddamn Lazy Susan the finishing touches. It seems I would have the house about finished now if I hadn't tangled with that bitch. She is a smart looker, however and maybe worth the time spent on her.

2/13/54 Pulpwood & woodwork and Layna & Karen - not a bad combination.

2/17/54 Much elated when it dawned on me that Paul [Laurence] thot Chris had done finishing in our house.

6/20/54 Hauled a big load of garbage to dump - that ended the wedding celebration!

12/30/54 He was eager to show it off, and as usual on such occasions he didn't do so well.

4/5/55 The designing of any piece of furniture is like giving birth to quintuplets. We usually manage somehow, but it isn't a normal delivery.

3/13/56 It is a well built utilitarian piece of equipment. I suppose some damned guide will drop it on a rock the first day it goes out on a trip.

6/6/56 Put Karen's boat in water. It leaked like a basket.

10/19/56 Home by 5 p.m. and cleaned every movable thing out of cruiser. Those painters won't get rich off her next year.

4/24/57 I cut a piece off of it to make a patch for a small hole. I am getting old. I laughed and walked away instead of taking axe and making more holes.

5/29/57 It took much cursing and some figuring before we were able to master the damned thing.

8/13/57 I miss Louie on these long trips. I used to play cards while he wheeled the boat. So far, I have not trusted either Jerry or Bill for the job. Poor management on my part.

9/22/58 Chore boy on Norway Island - and I think I could handle job as well as Johnny, with a little practice.

1/24/59 As I told the crew, the farmers must have got up around 7 a.m. to take a pee and in discovering it was only 5 below said "Hell, I might as well haul in a load of [pulp] wood!"

2/7/59 I worked a couple of hours and finished. Now I don't know if I felt better because I worked or worked because I felt better

2/10/60 ....my fears were well founded. The 41 should have been 47. I sure would have been a mad Swede if I had cut them wrong. Not sure if I should be mad at myself for being so dumb at measuring or pleased because I caught it

5/12/60 I told Layna that we were like a couple of farts in a mitten but she convinced me that all our troubles were not our own doing. That cheered me up!

7/28/60 Looks like I have survived another siege of abnormal activity.

12/10/60 This is the first time in my life I have been on a 40 hour week. I could learn to like it!

1/30/61 Instead, I keep outwardly calm, at a helluva effort, which is good training for my summer job.

5/23/61 Kids aren't the only ones who misjudge their capabilities.

5/26/61 They plan on putting buoys in Kabetogama. Maybe I'll get the job. Maybe it will amount to something. Maybe it will be a pain in the neck!

8/10/61 When it was all over, he ate a couple of tranquilizers. As near as I know, he did not pass them around to the others.

7/11/61 Home at 10 p.m. to find Tad at island. He won't go fishing with Crawford and me. If he had been an Indian, we would say he was unreliable!.

1/5/62 Snow plow went by during night and partially plugged our driveway. I went out about 9:30 - still 20° below, to clean it out. Somehow I got in the snow shoveling mood and kept right at it practically all morning. A big job. Even cleaned out behind house. Maybe I was thinking of the $2.00 that Clyde Martin charges for the job.

3/12/62 The Ramey Loader people (one of them young Ramey) hung around all day trying to sell their product. Of course every truck driver was a prospect. When young Ramey went out his companion said "Boy, is he nervous seeing all these trucks." I answered "Yes, he reminds me of a whore at an Elks' convention!"

3/21/62 They were all fouled up and I had a hard time [keeping] from blowing a fuse. Did some small sputtering, but not enough to make much of an impression.

12/28/62 Today in describing one of the top men in the organization "He is just like an alert football player in that he is always ready to pick up a loose ball and run with it. The hell of it is that you never know which way he will run, and your greatest concern is that he will kick it over your own goal posts!"

1/14/63 And the men up on the piles - I wonder that they don't freeze solid and fall off like a giant icicle.

5/7/63 On these occasions, I can't help but compare the repartee of these uncouth, uneducated laborers with some of the vapid conversation I have heard in the same setting.

9/4/63 Layna and I talked to REA crew about trees. I wanted to kill the bastards but knew it would not bring back our trees.

9/6/63 I am pooped but so is every other poor soul connected with this houseboat. Damn such unnecessary driving!

12/22/63 Almost forgot that I went out after lunch and cut a tree. A unique experience. I took the first decent one I saw!

1/7/64 Jack Ward, Swenson, and Buck in a long winded discussion of something they knew little about. I broke it up at 11:30. Felt they shouldn't use my time for such purposes.

1/8/64 He is fooling with an old campaigner there, and he might as well chew on one of the pulp piles.

3/27/64 I have learned from past experience that there is damned little we get away with in this world and can see no reason why this case is any different.

5/27/64 Damnation, but I meet a lot of men who hold rather important jobs that successfully hide what they have on the ball.

11/26/64 The damned furnace ran out of oil. We tipped up tank and got it going. I had to suck on pipe to get oil flowing. Got a mouthful of kerosene, a damn poor after dinner drink.

12/18/64 Her 16 hours a day working at NWI in summer is good training for the Xmas rush.

6/10/65 This was not a labor of love for our Norwegians. "Dr. Hvoslef would roll in his grave if he saw this." Said Chris. Layna replied "By now he has spun so often that one more roll won't make much difference." How true. There is little left of the original deal we made in 1945.

9/5/65 While at Dahlbergs about 1940, B.G. said "Why don't you and I trade jobs?" I told him "When you offer someone something it should be better that what he already has." Hansberger and I went thru same routine at table today. In each case, I should have added "You might have as much trouble with my job as I would have with yours."

12/6/65 I have never known two men who knew so damned much in their own right and had so little respect for the knowledge of other.

5/5/66 To cruiser where painters, mechanics, millwrights crawling over her like flies - and seemingly accomplishing as much.

9/11/66 We stopped at Bernice's new house and I am amazed, not so much as to what has been done, but rather why it was done.

9/20/66 My crowning remark, which all must have taken personally, "The trouble lies in the fact that most people who can't keep up have ambitions which exceed their capabilities."

12/8/66 New blood has to be pumped into this organization. Blood that has not been contaminated by experience.

12/30/66 At this moment, I feel that International Falls would have been better off had it been hit by an earthquake. Then the Red Cross and the Federal Government might have taken pity on us. As it is, there is no mercy.

1/6/67 He has a moron crew and genius bosses. He is squarely in between.

1/9/67 Peterson heard in Littlefork that Bob Faegre lost M & O to Hansberger in a poker game. Christ - I am almost ready to believe it.

5/14/67 Didn't even swear. This is not necessarily a good sign.

5/28/67 For a change of pace we went to Dahlbergs old barn and dug up a load of old rotted manure for Layna's flower bed. We are still taking crap from Gilda!

8/9/67 Despite what B.C.C says, experience does not have to be a handicap.

8/19/67 Should have done it years ago. On the other hand we now spent quite a little time and money making it easier for a dock boy who hasn't enough to do in the first place. I will appreciate it when I take over.

8/21/67 Piece by piece we are replacing the rotten wood on island. Too bad we can't do as much for ourselves.

3/26/68 Good God, how we worked that fall and winter! Walk, walk, walk from Dahlbergs to NWI and back, day after day. We must have been tough. I tell myself that whatever we have in this world, we have earned, and I am not kidding myself.

4/4/68 Johnny DeShaw was supposed to go to island to repair power line. Too cold. Hope it gets done before it gets too warm.

4/24/68 I requested a life jacket from the Coast Guard but was told that the Lamplighters were not eligible. They sent me a hard hat instead. Kee Rist!

6/12/68 Many odd jobs around NWI. I am trying to earn my keep, and some days do.

7/10/68 I got him alone in fishhouse and chewed hell out of him, knowing full well I could just as well talk to the ice maker.

7/11/68 "Drink is the curse of the working man" - and their bosses!

7/17/68 Jim was up on roof and said, "Here comes six people in a boat". I answered, "And they are all superintendents."

11/8/68 It took 15 years to get a solid driveway which had a few holes that needed patching. Now we have loose gravel over most of it - and I have a sore back.

7/12/70 Layna and I took this mixed up day in our stride. Not so with our kitchen help, altho Joan doesn't get too nervous despite her mother.

12/5/70 I finished putting trim around doors and windows. Uncle Olaf would not approve of my methods but Emil Johnson would.

1/9/71 After gang left, Layna and I (against my will) dug into the mountain of dirty dishes.

6/30/71 Bernice full of talk about all her activities. I could not help but compare it with her lack of activity when she was being paid here.

5/21/72 Hours and hours and hours of work staring us in the face at island. Some day the prospect of doing all of it will be too great - even as it did to the Hvoslefs, and we will give up.

5/26/72 Chop, chop, chop, rake, rake, rake, burn, burn, burn, putter, putter, putter. Good!

5/30/72 It looks good around NWI tonight. My back says it should.

6/7/72 To Ranier and picked up the other 15 hp Johnson. I was amazed at how much weight it had gained during the winter.

9/11/73 Was I stupid to be wrong in first place, or smart to discover my error?

10/6/73 Discovered there was no way I could put plastic tarp over it alone. Wind wrapped me up in it instead of boat. Gave up.

2/26/74 Had a strong feeling of inferiority when I craned my neck to see top of IDS building. Somebody designed and built it. It took me 3 days to build a few feet of wall around a toilet!

3/6/74 It boosted my ego to see him try to bore hole in stainless steel with drill running in reverse! Even a genius does dumb things occasionally.

3/13/74 I had chiseled the equivalent of a hole 10" by 9 feet. Not bad for an old man.

12/27/74 Felt like a scab later when I carried a box and beat a kid out of a job!

.4/20/75 They have done a good job there. That place, and Musket Inn, reminds me of what Vance used to say "Any carpenter can build a boys' camp - but let him go try to find the boys."

8/9/75 In a weak moment, I decided to put tent up. What a major undertaking that turned out to be. Aluminum poles in bad shape. Don't think they will stand another erection.

8/12/75 Much help by most present and the strain isn't all on Layna. Me - I stumble along doing the chores and mixing drinks. I can handle all that.

10/30/75 Vacuum cleaner salesman, McCourt, came at 7:30 and spent 2½ hours cleaning our rug. We successfully resisted his sales pitch - and he understood. A fine young man and we wish him luck.

2/1/76 It would take a lot of planning in order to do less than we did today.

4/15/76 Mosquitoes last night! I repaired both screen doors, Layna washed windows and put up screens. We are prepared now for the little bastards.

6/21/77 Getting gas hauled is like putting up ice in olden days. I never breathe freely until done.

9/16/77 Stopped and inspected Bern's development. It is stupendous. We wonder if she wonders as her friends wonder if she knows what she is in for.

4/1/78 I can understand how modern man can build an automobile - even understand somewhat the space program but can in no way grasp how early Britons built the building we saw today. What a remarkable bunch.

4/10/78 Finished at 8:30 and off to Fishbourne ruins of Roman Palace. A great job of restoration. Said I to Layna, "The Romans were clever people to build something like this but it took some clever Englishmen to put it back together since 1960 when it was found."

10/8/78 This looks like the very last load of stuff from NWI for 1978.- unless I go back and catch a boat load of fish!

11/2/78 Forgot the tag on counter and had to go back thinking, "Pa was right. If you don't have the brains in your head, you must have them in your feet".

12/20/78 Was reminded of one of my greatest bloopers - several years ago we put a rug in Layna's room. I cut the door off about ½ inch on the top end! I glued the piece back on and the second time got it right. If I had repeated that today I would have been a bit perturbed with myself.

3/23/79 He plans to tie a couple of huge pontoons on houseboat and float it over to Review Islands. He is a lot smarter than I if it works and a lot dumber if it doesn't.

9/19/79 Layna and I to inspect building on Williams' Island. A young carpenter in charge said "There are a lot of unexpected problems that come up in this island building." We agree - and glad that it is behind us.

May 1980 Special Data The only one who did anything for NWI was Carole who raked and raked. I am not complaining, just reminding myself that the best laid plans of Scots and Swedes often get lost in the shuffle.

6/3/80 We treated Louise to a can of beer when we came down into main house. It loosened her tongue (and maybe her brain) because she said she liked our place better than Musket Inn, yea, even better than Curtice Island. That's what made me wonder - still the talk was appreciated.

7/20/80 A tour of the 1½ acre island and all seemed to agree that there were many possibilities - most involving hard work.

3/17/81 Despite our colds (or maybe because of them) we had a long discussion concerning the fate of Norway Island. The Hvoslefs held onto it as long as they were physically able to take care of it. Have we reached that point?

7/13/81 Layna says she is tired of picking up after everyone. I believe her.

9/5/81 Robin and John willing and able to do the heavy work. All I did was to make a few suggestions and fall down a couple of times in dodging a falling tree

6/26/82 The rest of us did what we do best. Nothing of importance.

8/16/82 A restless night thinking about that damn storage shed. The only feasible solution was to hire somebody to haul whole damned works to the dump.

12/7/82 Don Thomas came to look at furnace at 8:30 a.m. He left at 10:30. We have a new motor on the fan and he has an extra $112.00.

11/1/84 A wild, cold day. Buck sweating out the buoy job. This day reminds me of my trip from Kettle Falls with Cliff Blais. I don't have to, nor am capable of that kind of activity. A decided plus for getting old.

11/4/84 Robin picked up the kids after supper. He had been to Ely where he arranged to go on a 2 week winter dog team camping trip in January. I am not going along.

12/28/84 He was at it less than 2 hours and when I asked him what we owed him he said "how about ten!" His father plows for nothing so I can't complain.

1/25/85 I dug out some 1944-46 diaries and read aloud to Sally. They told about the struggle to get NWI operating. Many memories - some not so fond - but all interesting.

8/16/85 As Buck said [referring to storm damage] "They have gone from devastation to a real mess."

10/15/85 He followed the instructions sheet and in a couple of hours had it working. It is magic and Buck is a magician.

10/6/86 After several days of prodding, two plumbers came to take the old Jungers furnace out of the basement. She was a faithful servant for 34 years. Not much that we prize on this earth does as well.

Chapter 10 - Travels

- *Travel was always a pleasure for my parents. In 1941 they had made a car trip with another couple from International Falls to California, with stops at as many national parks as possible. In 1949 they had the opportunity to travel from Cincinnati to New Orleans and return as guests of the captain of* The Delta Queen. *After they attained a level of financial independence they began to make extended trips. Although they made several other trips, to Florida, Vancouver, and New York, their favorite destination was Mexico where they traveled eleven times.*

11/11/49 We were full of talk about our trip, the biggest thing in the world to us, but spent most of evening listening to Beryl tell about Lee, their cat, and what happens in Dayton's bargain basement!

10/19/57 Stayed at Arrowhead, a quiet place. "Menopause Manor", Layna called it.

11/17/58 It seems like these West Chicago people never eat out in their own home towns. They always go somewhere. Must be the same urge that causes us to fish on the other side of the lake.

11/14/59 There were 55,000 people in the stands, and altho I saw many parkas, there were also many bare heads - empty too, I would say.

11/16/60 [Phoenix Scottsdale area] As near as I can see, a strange breed of American millionaires have been sold on building in this area. The worse the site, the more desirable - and expensive. Some of the lots perched on the side of a rock mountain sold for $20,000. The houses are all in the $100,000 plus bracket. All the nuts are not locked up.

4/25/66 A so called documentary, and they tried to do a good job, but I did not see the Mexican people there that impressed me so when we were with them.

1/16/68 The kid wanted 7 pesos, Black said 5 was enough, and we settled for 10. We are great bargainers!

1/17/68 In a weak moment, I bought a pair of haraches. They cost 18 pesos and tonight, 1 peso will take them. If no offers made, I'll give them away.

1/27/68 He showed considerable irritation with a Mexican bartender who was so dumb he couldn't speak English. Oh, my dear countrymen!

1/28/68 to the Plaza in evening where we watched boys promenading one way and girls the other. Occasionally they paired off. We saw the results of 1966, 1965, 1964, 1963, etc. All damned cute kids.

2/8/68 You need more study and practice, Johnson, not more books.

1/14/69 The climax came when I got a sudden call to the biffy at restaurant and learned that there was no paper. I took my trusty pocket knife and cut a chunk out of the roller towel. I did it and now, 12 hours later, I am still glad.

1/25/69 Our hotel rather nice, very new and modern, but the noisiest damned place on earth, not excepting Vietnam.

3/5/69 It was so damned dark that I ate all my brook trout, fins, tail, bones and all.

3/20/69 Many seemed happy that I was back. I am sure many more didn't know we had left.

12/5/69 A great welcome from Mr. and Mrs. Andreas and off we went on time. We were supposed to talk NWI but all they wanted to talk about was all the people they had seen at the dinner who knew us.

12/7/69 Good Lord, what an affluent society we live near - not in.

12/8/69 We circled for about 20 minutes while I visualized hundreds of others around us, all potential crasher inners.

1/24/70 We pulled over to the shoulder and had the pleasure of having our fellow motorists splash slush over us as we changed the tire.

2/25/70 We walked the beaches and shelled. What a profusion of life! I feel smaller and smaller. The Grand Canyon overwhelmed me. Now I feel akin to the tiniest shell.

3/3/70 A good motel for $10.00 but a horrible meal for $4.00

2/20/71 We left our "port in a storm", the New Yorker, at 8:30. If it was a matter of staying there or go home we would have headed north.

3/14/71 We were happy to learn that there were 7 other couples staying there. Some of them were very disgruntled. We weren't. It was just like NWI in 1945.

3/16/71 He criticized the Mexicans for never finishing anything and I jumped right down his throat. His last remark as we left was "I know what I'm talking about, and you don't". I had one consolation. He was obviously so upset that his lunch was spoiled.

4/2/71 It is hard to grasp the concept of a population explosion after the past two days. We have driven more than 1000 miles over desert as far as the eye will reach on either side.

3/2/73 A dozen or so Mexican caballeros offered their horses for the 2 kilometer trip into the valley but Layna's butt still sore from 1956 trip in Montana.

3/10/73 This might not be the jet set but it isn't exactly Piper Cub, either.

2/26/77 There were thousands of them (kids & parents, both) and no screaming from either. A well mannered lot and it reaffirms my faith in the future.

3/9/77 A fellow traveler told us of a sign he saw over toilet in drought stricken California "If it's yellow, let it mellow, if it's brown, flush it down." Can use that at home.

3/24/78 We are getting a strong case of Englanditis. I told Layna that I will probably see some ruin over there and say "This is where Montezuma built his last Castle!" My head is full of information - and misinformation.

4/1/78 Tara coughing, my knee aching, Layna stiff, Carole yawning, Byrne a bit pooped but I am sure all very, very, happy.

4/16/78 Byrne made prize remark of trip. "All I ask is that you understand my confusion!"

2/2/80 We bought 2 petunias, potted. I asked the merchant what they were called in Spanish and she answered "pee-tune-i-a!" We learn something every day!

2/21/80 We sat at table for a full hour after - most of talk in rapid Spanish, altho everyone there talked a fair amount of English. We have been exposed to this before and wonder at it. However, it is their home and it is their privilege to speak any language they wish. Memories are made of these experiences.

3/11/80 She talked steady about her trip out west. I seriously doubt if she knows we went to Mexico.

9/2/80 All of them have traveled extensively to far off places. Mexico seems close to Ericsburg when I hear them talk.

1/21/81 The stores all doing a rushing business but Garcias the most popular. A real gold mine. I can just imagine what was going thru that fat Mexican's head as he played a tune on his cash register-Sucker Yankee, Sucker Yankee!

1/24/81 It was a super barbecue sandwich joint. Very primitive but good if you didn't look too hard at the peeling paint held to the ceiling by cobwebs.

2/15/81 To church with Jean. As was the case several years ago, the minister asked the new guests to stand and introduce themselves. A cold breeze thru the place when I said "Don and Layna Johnson, International Falls, Minnesota".

2/17/81 Estero Island cluttered with condos- all claiming their own piece of the beach. The only reason that the north end does not tip into the sea is that the south end balances it.

2/19/81 Jean showed slides of her trip to Holy Land. They were good. Sure made me wonder why anyone would want to fight over that God forsaken sand pile.

Chapter 11 – Political & Legal

- *Don was never anything other than a Republican in the national elections, but never active except to vote. Certainly his thinking was influenced by Bror Dahlberg and the nearly unanimous views of the executives that he knew on the houseboat. I can't believe that he would have been pleased with the current state of his party.*

- *I believe that it would have been tragic if he had much need for lawyers. They would probably have driven him completely crazy.*

3/18/48 Wallace made speech in answer to Truman. I came to the conclusion that one or the other is either badly misinformed or a damned traitor!

11/2/48 Republicans had been so damned cocky the past month that they had us all believing it was a forgone conclusion that Dewey was our next president. I didn't vote!

11/3/48 Radio full of smart commentators who can now explain how Truman won the election. Christ! They are as bad as fishermen.

7/29/49 When Richardson got me alone he said, "Don, what kind of a president would Stassen make?" I am now giving opinions on affairs of state!

11/22/49 Also very interested in discussions by crew on world and national affairs. Those boys not so dumb. Lack of education tempers their judgment, maybe for the better in some cases!

1/3/50 it made me realize more how our "American Way of Life" is wrapped up in governmental red tape - I will probably live to see the day when we will all be choked by it.

12/28/50 Interesting talks with Byrne on international situation, which neither of us understand, which means we ought to be in Washington with the rest of the know nothings!

6/7/51 A common enemy makes (as in politics) strange bedfellows.

3/12/53 we got our income tax lined up. I hate like hell to pay it - but somehow it doesn't seem quite as bad to give it to the Republicans.

4/3/57 I sure get mad at the state deal - especially the surtax for the Goddamn Korean veterans, who, if they had an ounce of brains, would know that they too are being milked by the politicians.

1/20/59 Eisenhower making a desperate effort to balance budget but our Democratic congress will see that he doesn't. I am not criticizing them as Democrats - just as politicians. A Democrat president would be having the same trouble with a Republican congress. God help poor little me and the other 160,000,000 like me that are put in the squeeze. If they can't balance 77 billion in times like these, what will we do when it gets tough?

4/9/63 I feel our government is bleeding us dry and altho writing to congressman Blatnik and Senator Humphrey would do as much good as putting my complaints in a bottle and throw them into the Rainy River (which flows to Hudson's Bay), by God, I can scream about it in my own home. There.

4/12/63 Those Canadians are sure raising hell with their country in the name of progress. Down deep, I realize they have no choice. I just hate to see them cut a tree! Nuts - sounds like Oberholtzer, which I am not.

5/23/64 A beautiful speaking voice - full of sage utterances, known by some as platitudes, but effective.

3/23/65 Grissom and Young took off and sailed in orbit for 3½ hours. All details including the "why" way beyond my comprehension. I am reading Leopold's *Sand County Almanac*. That I can understand - partly!

12/26/65 [Joan Baez] The poor girl is only saying "Surely in a so called civilized society, there must be a better way than war to settle an argument!"

3/9/66 God damn a system that stirs up a new war for every generation.

4/8/66 Much good conversation on serious subjects. Can't say I learned much except that Dr. Jernberg is not worried too much about deficit spending and inflation. Buck is. So is Johnny. I don't know.

11/22/66 It is a type of rebellion I am too old to join. I do not resent the rebels as so many of my generation do.

2/19/67 Not too much trouble shoveling out altho my Japanese boots leaked badly and my feet got soaked. (They, the Japs, sure won the war).

2/22/67 Taxation is not a fun subject. Bud Herrem, who does not own a goddamn square inch of property says, "Well, somebody has to pay". It reminded me of the old Bill William's record we had back in 1919 at Buck Lake. A Bengal tiger was loose in the streets. Said Bill, "Somebody has to go and get that cat. Yes, somebody has to go. It is a wonderful chance for somebody. Somebody else - not me!".

3/11/68 Listened (and watched) U.S. senators cross examine Dean Rusk on conduct of Vietnam war. A stupid thing for our government to air its troubles before the world.

4/5/68 Johnson pleads for law and order. Leaders of both black and white try to sell people, black and white, on the idea that King preached a gospel of non-violence. The violence goes on.

6/13/68 Harold Stassen flew in and was interviewed by TV cameraman. It is 20 years ago, 1948, when he was guest on houseboat, running for president. Well, he is still running - further behind each try.

12/31/69 The greatest feat of the 60's was to send a man to the moon - while over 30,000 Americans died in Vietnam.

1/15/70 Why, oh why can't the intelligence that built the freeways and sent men to the moon and back be used to settle our social problems?

11/4/70 Kennedy, in his victory speech, said he was for Peace and got a great ovation. Now wasn't that something?

12/10/70 I don't know why he[Nixon] should ever talk to those bastards who obviously are not there to learn anything but rather to tie him in verbal knots.

1/12/71 From what I have been reading lately there are a lot of "public servants" dumber than me.

2/4/71 Our astronauts due for moon walk during night and I think we are with the majority of our fellow countrymen when I say "So what?" There are many serious problems to be solved ahead of that one.

1/21/72 I had finished a rough draft of Federal tax. We will pay so much less than last year that I am afraid Nixon will have to make another state of the union speech.

1/23/72 Well, maybe the powers that direct it all feel that John Q. Public should get a little respite from the blathering of the politicians. The campaign of 1972 will last longer than the football season and we will get just as fed up.

2/5/76 Layna to Republican Women's meeting. They are as scarce in Koochiching County as a Protestant in Mexico.

2/23/76 A couple of local lawyers, Jerry Shermoen and Joe Boyle talked for 2 hours and the important thing I learned was that we are at the mercy of the lawyers.

4/13/76 It went well enough, altho I couldn't explain why a vest type life preserver was necessary in a big boat but a cushion would do in one less that 16' - also a rowboat or canoe!

7/15/76 It was followed by a more sobering one by Carter - so sober that this poor old tired Swede fell asleep. Will read about it in paper tomorrow.

10/22/76 Home for dinner and then watched last of the 3 debates between Carter and Ford. Both very cautious, not wanting to repeat former blunders. Not much post debate discussion between Jernbergs and Johnsons. I think we all feel that we are not backing a real champion

3/2/79 Visited until noon, had lunch, then gals went shopping leaving the men folk to settle affairs of the world, a job we handled as well as Carter and Co.

3/18/79 He told of the terms of the divorce and from our standpoint, he is getting rooked. The old saying came up "Alimony is the screwing you get for the screwing you got!"

7/14/79 Much money involved and where there is money there is greed - and not only by the heirs. The lawyers have been nibbling for many years and now are about to get at it in big chunks. Once more I say "Thank you, dear Ober, for not getting us involved."

3/17/80 Gene talked about Ober's estate. Damn near a horror story.

4/1/80 Primary elections in Wisconsin and Iowa. Reagan and Carter heavy winners. What a Goddamn pity if we should have to vote for either one of those lightweights in November.

9/21/80 I watched Reagan - Anderson debate. They sounded like a couple of politicians!

1/17/81 Much talk about hostage release but I doubt if anyone is optimistic at the moment. They have Uncle Sam by the testicles and won't let go as long as he doesn't threaten to fight back.

9/14/81 We are babes in the woods in dealing with lawyers.

11/1/82 Last day before election and TV is full of candidates making their final pitch. Much to do about the amount of money some of them are spending. Tomorrow we will learn which ones bought their way into office.

12/14/84 I came away thinking, "Those lawyers sure must have a racket to put on a show like that."

1/1/85 Everyone gone by 9:00 leaving us alone to watch TV tell us about rape, murder, bombings, traffic deaths, child abuse - on & on. HAPPY NEW YEAR!

7/7/86 The documents were more wordy than the old ones to the tune of $250. Doctors and lawyers don't come cheap.

Chapter 12 - Nature

- *Don was a keen observer and lover of nature and often was led to comment on its wonders.*

12/7/44 Saw flight of small birds - about as big as chickadees but more streamlined. They passed about 35 feet up. Hundreds of them - their combined chirping sounded like steam escaping from kettle.

3/14/45 Just as we rolled out the last log, the northern lights came out in all their glory. They well paid us for working so late.

11/16/45 Today we started our fall navigating - always full of wondering how we will make it, but I guess the real wonder is why we don't stay home until it gets better.

2/6/49 A most thrilling sight when gale of about 40 mph came up out of dead calm and whirled fresh snow off of island trees, looked like they were on fire.

5/15/49 Flying weather perfect. Soft green of poplar and birch leaves against deep green of the pines made a most interesting pattern.

7/21/49 Terribly rough ride home - the worst I have ever seen Rainy Lake. I was plenty damned worried, but everyone seemed to have plenty of confidence in me. Seems at times that I am like [Captain Horatio] Hornblower, scared to death but inspiring everyone else - too damned bad I can't kid myself the same way.

5/4/50 Three weeks ago every third person I met talked about the weather. Two weeks ago it was every other one. Now it is a "must" in all conversations

6/4/51 A rare June day. Soft white clouds would billow up from horizon and darken before they got very high. Then they would disappear to be replaced by more of the same.

4/29/52 Sunday the Falls was the hottest spot in U.S. with much of South in the 50's. The pessimists are saying "We will pay for this yet", and I answer "Goddamn it, we have paid for this!"

5/4/56 Paul Anderson wanted to get me to predict lake opening and I told him that neither Don Johnson or anyone else knew anything about it.

5/5/52 I had fully planned on going to *Mando* when the wind went down but it didn't, so I didn't!

5/11/56 The battle of the last 3 days of wind vs. ice reminds me of a lumberjack brawl. Wind beat ice with its south wind punch, then north wind punch and then east. Ice was down on the floor last night and today wind put the boots to her with the strongest blow yet. Straight from the west. It was a coup de grace for sure.

5/17/56 Snow flakes like Walter's pancakes covered the ground.

9/27/57 Big bull moose standing by the house on Dunmore Island. He stayed for 15 minutes while gang got cameras out of bags and loaded them for pictures. He posed in a most professional manner.

10/31/58 Man may be an important creature in the cities, but little old me, sitting on my dock at Norway Island, felt no more necessary to the scheme of things than the owl who hooted across from Keyes Island or the fish that splashed near ours.

2/8/60 This winter, so far, doesn't know how to get rough.

5/20/61 As the sun slipped below the horizon, the moon came into its own. So did the loons. The Rabbit Island pair got in communication with their friends and relatives at Rat River, Stokes Bay, Camp Bay and no doubt they were in tune with some at Brule Narrows, which my feeble human ears could not detect.

5/21/61 I was awake at 3:15 when the first white throated sparrow greeted the morn. A faint flush of daylight was all he needed to get going - me too!

8/17/61 Wind and weather no respecters of big shots.

6/9/64 Saw blue heron who looked more miserable than I felt.

11/24/64 About rabbits. They have been practically extinct in this area for about 3 years. One year's good hatch, however, and they will "cover the earth".

3/4/65 Where did man originate? In Africa 1,750,000 years ago says Prof. Leaky. I'll take his word for it. Some of us haven't come very far from our predecessors.

12/2/65 I began to feed the birds today and many of last years flock must have been on hand for the opening. They came when I rattled the can.

7/14/68 Our little birds are hanging to their nest and 3 young. They inspire me!

7/68 Special data - I know that man is supposed to pray for strength to an Almighty. I got mine from our little bird.

11/16/58 we ran to Horricon Marsh to see goose flight. It was there. We even saw one get shot. Also thousands of luckier ones.

3/18/70 Temperature in high 30's. Clear sky, no wind. If we had many days like this there would be few Swedes in Florida.

5/3/70 Small birds twittering, loons calling, mallards quacking, crows cawing, ice rustling. Great to be alive.

5/29/72 A mallard hen had built a nest near our cabin before we moved up here. Now she flies off almost every time we go by. I am afraid the eggs will spoil. Not yet, however. I tried one. It looked good enough to eat.

11/2/72 I saw mink towing one of our lost ducks along shore. Thought it was an albino beaver.

9/7/73 Watched a squirrel at our landing cutting off pine cones which dropped in the water. A true exercise in futility.

5/9/74 The sun burst out (after a cloudy day) and I decided to go to island. Did what I do best, fart around with a small boat on Rainy Lake.

7/21/75 A pigeon showed up on our island!

PS It stayed until Aug 1. A capsule on its leg indicated that it was a racer. It must have come in last after loafing on NWI for 10 days.

7/26/75 Our "retarded" mallard left her nest today. I first saw her on it on June 1, which means she was on it for at least 8 weeks. Something wrong with her timing mechanism. I broke a rotten egg two weeks ago.

9/23/75 I quit feeding the ducks. They are on their own. I don't want them to depend on me until freeze up. It has added a lot to my summer's enjoyment of NWI, more than the $28 we spent for feed.

6/22/76 Today we hauled debris that has gathered to different pile and burned same. A lot of extra work because of a duck that could be a mental case.

8/20/76 Said he "What was your greatest concern during the worst part of the storm?" "The trees", I answered. "How about your own safety?" "Not at all, I figure that the trees are more important than Don Johnson!"

10/14/76 Our weasel still with us. I first saw him when he ran across yard with ½ my sandwich in his mouth. Well, I don't know anyone I would rather share my lunch with.

4/12/77 I saw a rabbit across the road. A real thrill, they are so scarce that they should be on endangered species list. Hope he can find the one I saw back of house last fall and they can go into production.

9/6/77 The "security lights" make night travel on the lake extremely hazardous.

1/12/79 Emil Johnson used to tell about a winter so cold that when the horses were taken out of the barn they took one breath and dropped dead. Their lungs were frozen solid!

5/20/79 Yesterday I put out a can of corn in feeding place for mallards. There were <u>3</u> drakes there when we came today. Surely they are from last year's brood. How do they do it!

9/23/79 Said Ruth "I never expect to get closer to heaven on this earth!" THANKS!

11/5/79 I have made friends with a couple of Canadian jays, also on speaking acquaintance with several squirrels. The ravens keep raving, waiting for the deer guts that I don't deliver.

4/10/81 The 25 mph wind raised the dickens by blowing the leaves around- mostly back where they came from.

7/13/84 I got a big charge out of them diving for corn near lower dock. It doesn't take much to amuse me.

2/20/85 A spring like day. Even the woodpeckers rap a new tune.

4/12/86 We did not rake the leaves last fall and they did not go away during the winter.

Chapter 13 – Environment

- *I find little reference to the environment in the early years, but he was never comfortable with its destruction or desecration. I would call him somewhat of a "small footprint" environmentalist. He certainly had little quarrel with the forest cutting practices of the M & O Paper Company, but when it came to cutting logs for our cabins, he made sure that he took few trees from any area.*

3/22/74 Had I met him [Sig Olson] to preach me conservation instead of the ranting of Oberholtzer, I would have had a different perspective - and a different life.

4/29/74 In p.m. we took ride to Rainy and Big Fork rivers. Saw where vandals had burned picnic table. Wish we hadn't.

5/25/74 Robin & Karen in canoe, Layna and I in rowboat. We saved 39 drops of gas, which is our contribution to the energy crisis. More than most people.

1/24/76 The Federal Fish and Wildlife are considering making a giant refuge for timber wolves in Minnesota, Wisconsin and Michigan. The report said that if there are not enough deer to feed the wolves they will shut off the season for hunters. That stirred up a howl.

9/25/76 Also donated $500 to Kabetogama Sportsmen to help in their fight against rough fish. To me it was like giving $500 to Boise to help clear up Rainy River.

9/76 Special Data Because of forest fire danger, the DNR has closed all northern 2/3 of state to hunting <u>and</u> fishing. This dumb Swede has a hard time understanding how an old man out in a boat is a fire hazard.

12/16/76 The Federal gov't has a "Recovery Plan" that has made the whole north country see red. One of the more ridiculous suggestions: "In event the deer herd drops to point where it won't feed the wolf population it may be desirable to introduce the woodland caribou!" Loving God!!

2/25/78 One quote from John Ridd, is speaking of wildlife "everyone of them was aware that we (man) desolate more than replenish the earth." Written 1875.

4/15/80 She said that she was writing an article on what the natives of the area think of the Company. It will be interesting to see how she will misquote me.

7/28/80 I would lie like hell if I said I wasn't relieved to see them go. The ecologist talk about the frail ecological structure of this rocky area. Well, this place isn't the same after being trampled on by 30 people.

11/18/82 Almost forgot that Dennis Johnson, a freelance writer from Mpls came to pick our brains about Oberholtzer. I am afraid that we didn't paint the same picture that the other worshipers did.

10/31/85 Dioxin, dioxin, dioxin. The newspapers and TV news full of it. Well, it takes the pressure off of the local economy.

Chapter 14 – Voyageurs National Park

- *I find little else in these journals that was as conflicting for Don than the establishment of Voyageurs National Park. Half of his best friends were strongly in favor of the park and the other half just as strongly against. His opposition was based on three things. He had visited Grand Canyon, Yosemite and a number of other national parks, so he had an image of the grandeur of those parks; he believed that if the projection of number of visitors set forth by the advocates came true, the environment could not survive; and finally, he had hunted those burned over hills for most of his adult life and could not recognize their value.*

- *Many years later I was visiting with Barb West, the park superintendent and told her of Don's objections to the park, including its lack of grandeur. She said, "Obviously he was never in the Everglades." To which I could only reply, "Point taken."*

4/29/63 Much antagonism against Harley Hanson, the state biologist. After meeting I told him "It has occurred to me after listening to this gang that the professional biologist has the same problems as a prostitute. Too much amateur competition."

12/23/63 We got into discussion of Voyageurs park, but Lou the only one who shouted. No decision.

9/19/64 Oberholtzer only one with guts enough to raise a voice in favor of proposal - and he used his time to say he was ashamed of his friends and neighbors for their conduct - and got a good hand!

10/4/67 Aldo Leopold summed it all up when he said,"All conservation of wilderness is self defeating, for to cherish we must see and fondle, and when enough have seen and fondled, there is nothing left to cherish." And this was written before the advent of plastic bags, beer cans and aluminum foil! Man's armament to destroy nature has increased a hundred fold in the past few years. What will the future bring? [Rainy River Reflections]

2/16/70 We drove to Everglades Park, arriving about noon. We walked the trails and took a 2 hour boat trip. All agreed that there was no wonder the Park Service wanted our area.

7/21/71 He asked me if I had heard of big deal concerning Voyageurs Park at Kettle Falls on Aug. 7. Before he could go further I said "Allan, I was confirmed in Lutheran Church when I was 12 years old (actually I was 15) and haven't been in one since (a little exaggeration). I have been praying for a 40 mph wind for the seventh of August ever since I heard about this deal. If I get it, I'll join the first church I walk into." I didn't faze him. He asked me if I would take 4 people to Kettle Falls and I agreed to do it!

1/19/72 To "seminar" at night to hear Sig Olson and Dickerman tell us how goddamn lucky we were to have a park and what we can do to make it a great one. At coffee later, I got a nose bleed and decided that I was allergic to bulls**t.

1/27/72 Our conversation confirmed our opinion of Myrl Brooks. A high class man who will handle a difficult problem very well if left alone. He does not need any more "help" like he got from that ass Dickerman at the last seminar.

9/13/72 My prayers were answered this morning. It rained on Gov. Anderson's Voyageurs Park party of about 40 people. My medicine not strong enough to keep it raining all day, however.

10/26/72 Not my kind of a deer country, however. Think I'll stick to the peninsula until Uncle Sam kicks me off - maybe longer.

1/16/73 Myrl Brooks there to give us lowdown on National Park. Didn't hear much that I did not already know but a few eye openers. They, too, are worried about opposition from environmentalists when they start to dig up nature in effort to build park.

6/10/75 On to Voyageurs Park hearing where we heard the usual gobbledygook. The only bright spot in program came when Woody Ewald was called on for comment and said "I had a question when I came but I won't ask it because nobody knows nothing"!

11/13/78 To Voyageur's Nat'l Park meeting. They were looking for input - AND GOT IT! A hostile crowd cheered the opponents and booed the proponents. I don't see much coming out of it all.

9/25/79 They got $75,000 for their Black Bay place and tickled to death over deal at the time. Now the lawyers for other property owners are questioning the appraisals and getting, in some cases, more than double the first offer. 'Twas ever thus.

10/13/79 According to him, the great majority of the natives were for the park. That ain't the way we saw it - "and we were right there".

8/26/83 We went for a ride to Four Island Resort, the proposed headquarters for the Park. Somebody blundered.

Chapter 15 – Aging

- *Although Don made many comments about aging, he certainly aged gracefully.*

4/6/48 [Don's birthday] Another sign of old age - I'm getting more critical - movies, radio, comic books, etc. Also of myself!

3/30/56 I learned that I had cut the uprights all exactly 1/8" short. Took it very calmly. A sign of old age.

2/1/59 To think that after 86 years, she has to be put into the hands of strangers because none of us can be bothered. It seems as bad as the Eskimos when they move off and leave the old and helpless to freeze or starve! Lucky is the one who cashes in their chips before they reach that state.

3/21/59 Right now I earnestly hope that my end will come more swiftly. Maybe when the time comes it will be less important.

10/3/69 Stopped at Kelliher to see Ben Haskell in rest home. Said he, "The last time I saw you, you were on your way to Vietnam." I told him I decided to go duck hunting instead and he seemed satisfied.

7/3/72 To me, after listening to him, there was only one answer. She is acting like a typical 82 year old. I told him so but he was not completely satisfied. I can't help but wonder if I will live to become a problem with our kids.

4/6/76 [Don's birthday] Layna gave me an electric Timex watch. She must have been noticing how often I have forgotten to wind my old one lately. More signs of senility.

6/4/76 She will be 86 years old soon and I think she should be entitled to a few idiosyncrasies. Hope that the Johnsons, if they live that long, retain their faculties as well as she has.

7/3/76 Much talk - I find myself contributing less and less as I grow older. I am sure now that I will not develop into a garrulous old man - maybe just the opposite.

8/15/76 My distance perception failing at night, especially in docking, another sign of old age.

7/4/77 I am working at not becoming a garrulous old man and at times feel I might be overdoing it. Maybe people will call me surly!

11/7/77 I told Erle about Mrs. Dahlberg's story about the 80 year old whores in Paris who are so good in bed because they figure each lay might be their last. Is that what keeps you going, Johnson?

1/1/78 There was a time when I could miss writing in my diary for a full week, then sit down and fill the pages. Now I find it difficult to remember what happened yesterday.

1/31/78 Said he "Marie gets some of the damnedest ideas." I told him "At her age (87) you should be happy she gets any ideas at all!"

5/23/78 My knee hurts but bearable. Layna's cold slow to improve We are getting old. Aw, shut up!

7/3/78 Old people get worse and I try to avoid it in my own behavior - Goddamn, but some of my old acquaintances are tiresome talkers.

2/24/79 Much laughter when I told our new friends (who had asked about car top carrier) "there is something really fantastic about that deal" - and then couldn't remember what it was. Still can't!

3/27/79 How lucky a sick old man is to have a healthy wife to take care of him. I will soon be of their number.

10/20/79 When he left, we both noticed that he had repeated himself a lot. Said Layna, "I think he is a little senile." "Who isn't?", said I.

12/13/79 A card from Helena LaFave said that she had celebrated her 80th birthday last fall. Said she, "Now I can do anything I please and can blame it on old age!"

3/10/80 Old Man Jaffray - on his 80th birthday on the *Mando* said "I haven't an enemy in the world. I've outlived them."

5/4/80 Layna heard Reverend Schumacher's sermon in which he talked about how sad it was to watch an old man grow older. She is sure he meant me - and I can well believe it.

6/24/80 I had occasion to think of old Deitrick who worked one year at Dahlberg. He was proud of his capacity to work. In his heavy German accent he would say "I am zevendy do years old" Lord but that seemed ancient.

8/17/80 Many of our peers say "Wouldn't you like to be 20 years old again?" Heaven forbid.

9/12/80 As I grow older, the outboards get heavier, the space under the floor joists of all the cabins is less and the nights are darker for boat travel.

4/2/82 We both noticed that Clara repeated herself a lot - a characteristic of older people. Let it be a warning to you, Johnson.

10/11/82 They left in a cold drizzly night. How many times did we do likewise - and God, how I would hate to do it again.

12/12/83 96 years old and senile. Well, he was a tough old bugger, especially when he was fly fishing for bass - with D. Johnson on the paddle.

12/24/83 I could have easily reached him with my foot but didn't. A sure sign of old age.

7/26/84 We will miss them, for my part because of the implication that they can't be there alone. Clint gets only 2 weeks vacation, so their time on Rainy Lake is really limited. Maybe George's diabetes and my Parkinsons, together with health problems of Layna and Ardys will take care of that sooner than we think.

7/30/84 Tad's father, 83 years old, sat right in middle of confusion. I hope I don't last that long.

1/13/85 I dream an old man's dream - and it is good!

3/2/85 I was about to eat a fork full of green beans when I spilled a couple in my lap. I said "Damn" and Sarah, who misses nothing, said "Think nothing of it, Grandpa, it is just a sign of old age."

8/24/85 I almost choked when he told the 75 year old man and 63 year old woman to "go forth, be fruitful and multiply!"

2/15/86 Layna gave the Senior Citizens some poems to be used in their quarterly paper. They all pertained to old folks losing their memory. I find that stuff very un-funny.

9/26/86 You, like ourselves, have reached the point when the comforts of home outweigh traveling to far away unknown places.

Chapter 16 – Medical & Health

- *Aside from two hernias, one prostate surgery, one broken leg and his Parkinsons Disease, Don had an essentially healthy life. He was, however, a keen observer of the medical profession.*

1/15/49 Nose still dripping at the rate of one pint to the hour.

4/4/49 Sam fed us rest of gallon can of beans he opened yesterday. Human stomach a wonderful thing - I hope!

1/1/51 Layna and I on diet again, that belly getting too big. Over indulgent during holiday season caused us to make decision. Here is how I can sum up that period. Ate altogether too much, drank a little too much, slept not near enough!

3/3/51 Measles false alarm, hell. She looks like a speckled trout.

3/25/52 Now that I have taken 6 pills (at $.55 a piece) I feel better. The words of old Dr. Hvoslef keep ringing in my ears however "How do you know you wouldn't have been better without that junk?"

3/29/52 but I can think of nothing worse in the world than to be tied to a sub-normal child. The greatest joy of parenthood is watching a child grow - physically and mentally. It would be hell otherwise.

12/11/54 She made a classic remark when she showed us some pills. "I wouldn't take these darn thing, because I am not afraid to die, except I want to live until spring. I hate to think of lying in that cold mausoleum all winter!"

4/17/56 If I bend over it hurts to straighten up. Will have to learn to stay bent.

4/25/56 Layna outwardly calm thru it all. What a gal! Anyone else would have killed me to put me out of my misery or left me - or both!

6/22/56 The Goddamn doctors sure do things to people - and it isn't all good.

1/31/57 Layna sick as a rabbit this morning. She doesn't mess around when she gets sick, it really puts her down.

12/14/58 Called Ma. She says she never would have got so near 100 if she hadn't eaten lutefisk!

12/19/58 Another day of dysentery and I don't like it. Only compensation, [Bob] Lessard looks worse than I feel. He think he has ulcers. Maybe cancer. He knows he has diarrhea.

12/30/58 I didn't go completely off my rocker, but sure can see how it can happen.

1/16/59 Dr. Solomon diagnosed appendicitis and he will operate tomorrow. The irony of all this is that Bob went to Dr. Hanover last week and was told he had an "allergy". God protect the poor layman from the medical profession. One does not have to be very bright to realize that either Solomon or Hanover is way off base in this case.

2/9/60 As I said to Dr. Lysne once in describing Helen, Dahlberg's cook, "If I saw an animal in the woods looking that bad, I would shoot it to put it out of its misery.

10/22/60 Layna has knit a couple of sweaters in that waiting room - and there isn't much wrong with her. God help the ones who are really sick.

4/16/62 He has changed from Dr. Hanover to Dr. Walter. Walter is working like hell to put back the weight that Hanover took off! God help anyone who finds himself at the mercy of those bastards.

5/1/62 I am sure that less food and more exercise is all that is necessary but it is a hard one to sell.

4/7/64 I made a blooper yesterday which caused me considerable pain today. I held my temper, did not throw a damned thing. There is some compensation on being 58 years old.

6/19/62 Damned if women aren't different in their thinking, a fact that is well recognized by psychologists but something the average man hates to accept!

1/29/64 The government cancer report, aimed at scaring hell out of every smoker, provided a bit of discussion when it came out two weeks ago, and now the American people are huffing and puffing their same old merry way.

12/13/64 Have had a chance to do a lot of thinking - some of it not very profound. Our normal body functions, which we take for granted most of the time (BMs and urination in particular), become life's greatest problems in a hospital.

12/29/64 [Layna] picked up Jim DiOnne and they tipped over [on snowmobile] when they approached highway - no casualties but I was sure glad my hernia was not aboard.

1/1/65 I watched a good share of all three [bowl games]. Can't say I feel in a position to criticize a drunk after that.

1/5/65 He [Dr. Thaller in *Calories Don't Count*] had a best seller going until it was discovered he was chief owner of a safflower oil plant. I never quite figured out how that should affect his diet.

12/18/65 Dr. Johnson feels that her [chest] pains have been muscular, a form of arthritis. I feel like the guy who spent $300 to have a private eye shadow his wife, only to learn that he was the only one she was sleeping with.

2/1/66 I think of my father at Buck Lake in 1921 - age 50. He pulled out most of his molars <u>by hand</u>. He walked the floor groaning as he did it. I can hear him yet. Tough Swede!

4/2/66 I wonder if this is inherited from my father, altho he got these spells only when he quit snuff.

7/5/66 Jurgenson (he looks like death warmed over and cannot drive) just bought a new Lincoln Continental. Well, I would not trade our Chevy (1962) and my health for their Lincoln and his health. (Sounds catty!)

3/2/67 Captain Billy Martin stopped in to see me at the office. He shook hands with both Bud and me and we had trouble writing checks for some time. He, at 83, is still a bone crusher.

12/24/67 I am as stuffed as the 20# turkey sent by Crawford Johnson.

9/27/69 He said he was happy that I was responding to treatment, gave me another shot, said to keep eating the pills and not to come back unless there was no improvement. God help anyone who is <u>really</u> sick!

10/10/69 The Mayo Clinic would probable have done no more but it is hard to have confidence in a doctor who looks about 20 years old.

10/13/69 Back to see Dr. Talsness at 2 p.m. Sat for 2 hours for a 2 minute visit. Said he, "My friend, you are doing fine. Come back next Saturday" - and was gone. No wonder they can handle a 100 people a day. God help anyone who is sick.

11/26/70 Home by 9:30 - stuffed. I keep thinking of Merrill Meigs who told us "Even a dog would not punish his stomach like that!"

6/8/71 I sat for 2 hours to see him [Social Security representative] - like waiting for a doctor. Old people and sick people should learn to wait gracefully.

5/20/72 I took it all very philosophically, in fact I even laughed when I saw water peeing thru a .22 sized hole near kitchen. Maybe it reminded me of my lost pressure.

10/27/72 Put non-skid treads on basement steps. Now all I have to worry about is the human element. It should take some doing to fall down those steps now.

11/21/72 Cliff reported that Lou overdid at health club and can scarcely walk. We are laughing (just a little) behind her back.

1/25/73 Animals aren't the only ones with homing instincts. Why should he want to leave the care and comfort of a clean hospital to crawl back into the hovel he calls home?

4/11/73 The creeping crud that came on me yesterday got creepier and crudier all day.

4/23/73 Fourth day in hospital - without a bowel movement. An enema took care of that. Of such things do we make news when we are put in confinement.

1/28/74 Layna's cough no better. There was a time when she would have gone to a doctor but the thought of sitting two hours in a waiting room is a deterrent.

3/23/74 John described the elaborate laboratory techniques and equipment at St. Mary's to keep this little one's body and soul together. A paradox in a land of legal abortion.

8/11/74 Got soaked, cut finger, bruised forearm, skinned shin, but still in one piece. I laughed when I came to that conclusion.

10/10/74 He examined my prostate, looked in my ears, found nothing startling, gave me a prescription and sent me home. Don't know if I should be elated that he found nothing wrong or depressed because my ailment escaped him. I still think I pee too often.

11/2/74 Cliff has ½ a stomach but eats twice as much as I do. Not complaining - just telling.

1/4/75 My nose running and I put on a sneezing fit for an interested audience in market.

4/28/75 She talked on and on about her recent surgery. I nodded and smiled like a damned Indian, not having heard anything previous about it. She talked about examinations in Duluth, anesthetists, doctors, nurses, care, recovery room, stitches and I was sure she had had nothing less than heart surgery. It finally came out that she had two bunions taken care of!

9/22/75 What do you say to a blind man [Wayne Judy] to cheer him up? I told about the rotten hunting and fishing that I had with George. That should help a little.

10/6/76 Layna and I to Falls for our "flu" shot. We stood in line outside of Union Hall for about 45 minutes in 35° weather. By that time, several hundred people were thoroly chilled and really needed the shots.

1/13/77 Received our rowing machine from Sears. It should help make my sluggish blood flow a little freer. Layna's too. I rowed around island a couple of times, fantasizing. I can plainly see that if it is to do me much good, I will have to take longer trips.

August 1977 Special Data Page: I woke up on the floor with a sore jaw where it had hit the night stand! This sleeping is dangerous business!

11/19/77 My knee, which gave me hell off and on all summer, was sore the first day out. I gave it a good talking to and it behaved well rest of time despite fact I walked a considerable amount.

12/12/77 That incident made me review my own situation and I came up with the following. "I think my cold makes me feel tough. I'll bet Wayne [Judy] hasn't felt as good as I do today in the past 5 years."

1/15/78 My urine still bloody at 10:00 p.m. What black thoughts run thru my head! Forgot that Dr. Walter said I was doing great. Even that wouldn't make my urine look any better.

1/18/78 A hospital is the best place to be when you don't feel well but the worst if you are O.K. I am O.K.!

5/17/78 Layna sneezing and coughing. Head plugged. She doesn't complain, except when Bern and I win at gin rummy.

10/4/78 Layna came back with report that Olive said that Gerald said that I was unsteady when I got out of my chair at meeting last Saturday. When I see him I am going to say that I let a wet fart, so had to be careful.

9/30/79 Buck's 53rd birthday. I don't need my few relatively minor aches and pains to tell me I am getting old. However, as I told Buck yesterday, "I may not be the man I once was but I am twice the man I was last spring!"

1/22/80 Fun in [Mexican] market with vendor of herbs. He even offered to improve my sex life. I told him I was afraid.

3/26/80 Started to take pills for my "shakes" this a.m. I checked my reflexes throughout the day and told myself I could detect a definite improvement! Psychologists must have a name for that kind of thinking.

5/6/80 Dr. Walter finally called. He seemed pleased with my progress. I felt better after talking with him. The Christian Scientists have something going for them.

6/15/80 Layna in misery with sore back and ribs. It was caused by bear hug administered by George a week ago. She will see Dr. Walter tomorrow.

8/14/80 I skinned my shin getting out of boat at Edwards dock. I manage to draw blood from this old frame practically every day.

11/21/80 I re-read article on Parkinsons and decided that I should quote my mother "I am 75 (74) years old. Surely I should have something wrong with me."

12/13/80 When we got to US customs, the officer asked if we had anything to declare. Layna said "Maybe two cases of the flu!". We shall see.

3/4/81 I try to be cheerful and a good companion but at times my concern for my health not very stimulating.

3/7/81 Went for a walk around Point of Pines. The dogs (some of them) have forgotten me. I got a couple of them with my walking stick.

3/14/81 At 4:30 my butt said I needed to exercise. Caught up with Jim and Baret and walked with them around loop. They don't put much zip in it so I doubt the value of it. Back to their house for coffee and a donut. No value there for sure.

3/15/81 Our colds in the running stage and we blew up a full box of Kleenex.

3/20/81 My mother's birthday. She is much in my thoughts. "I am 75 years old, Reverend, surely there must be something wrong with me!" She said that to Lutheran minister who wanted her to go to a faith healer for her arthritis.

4/7/81 I have had a dime sized scab near my left eye for about a year. Today Dr. Walter, with a minimum amount of fuss sliced it off. I should take up residence at clinic.

7/10/81 Fred Walter must have some magical powers because my bum leg didn't bother all the while he was here.

9/21/81 In keeping with my newfound awkwardness, I fell into dining area with an armful of wood. More scared than hurt. Layna too.

11/25/81 I worry about my Parkinsons, not knowing what the future will bring. Aw, shut up Johnson. You are developing into an Irene Case type of hypochondriac.

12/8/81 My stiff fingers could not relay the message sent down from my stiff brain.

1/21/82 Bannert a silent one except when cursing doctors and nurses.

1/14/83 The health book says that Parkinsons doesn't affect the mind. If that is true, I haven't got it.

4/27/83 We got a blow by blow account of all her bouts with the medical profession from the first slap on her rump to the 6 pills a day she is taking at the present time.

8/16/83 He had had polio when 18 years old and was cruelly crippled. A cheerful man and I can't help wonder how I would handle that kind of situation. Maybe I'll live long enough to find out.

1/7/85 My mind in a jumble. I am losing Dr. Walter, who apparently knows something about Parkinsons but just doesn't give a hoot, and gaining Helleloid, who cares but doesn't know a lot. I think I'll die a natural death.

4/6/85 [Don's birthday] I have to wonder as to what kind of shape I would be in were it not for the Parkinsons. I then get more rational and realize how well off I am despite the Parkinsons.

7/25/85 I used to kid about being the biggest coward in Koochiching County. Well, it is no joke now. I fear pain!

9/30/85 He prescribed some new pills, which I feel strongly are a shot in the dark, and sent me home - I am still sleepy.

1/14/86 I sure hope he knows what he is looking for, so that in the event he finds it, he can zero in on it.

3/14/86 I think I need an aspirin or a laxative or both. Layna eats her pills without comment.

3/19/86 The medical profession tells us to avoid stress but does its damnedest to drive us nuts.

3/21/86 She used a term "Bio Feedback" which sounded rather mysterious. I summed it up, after Ruth left, as a study of how your insides govern your outsides.

11/3/86 To see Dr. Burton. He was his usual friendly self. I wish that I had more faith in him. Or any of the others.

Chapter 17 – Death & Dying

- *Don was an agnostic and certainly had no expectation of an afterlife of any kind.*

4/27/54 I will soon reach the stage in life where ½ of my friends are in the ground, an interesting development that I haven't given much thot to up until now.

5/11/62 Said he "I'll be damned if I'll diet and lose weight - why should I feel sorry for you bastards who will be my pall bearers!"

5/20/65 I called Beryl who told me he had not been able to speak for 2 years. Was down to 87# at the end. I hope I drown before I get to that stage.

3/12/66 Our Molly, the life of the party, dying before our eyes. I have to learn to live with this sort of thing if I pull thru a few more years, but it is hard to take. Maybe it is not just Molly I feel sorry for. It is all of mankind.

5/6/66 We are sure to see much of this as we grow older, but it seems that the Grim Reaper pointed his bony finger at the wrong person when he took our Molly.

10/31/66 He has terminal cancer in his lungs - and looks it. God, what a helluva way to go. I hope I can follow Willie Halvorson when my turn comes.

12/2/68 Gina called to say John had passed away. Saw in paper where Leo Jung and Mabes Anderson were gone. This will be a chronicle of deaths until my own will be recorded - AMEN.

8/18/73 Jane gave us a blow by blow account of her father's bout with cancer. I can only hope that I a meet a sudden death if for only one reason. To keep them from cutting me up in small pieces.

5/7/74 Owen Miggins died last night and family wants me as a pall bearer. Now wasn't that a shock! He was full of plans for the future (including a visit to NWI) when I saw him just a month ago. On further thought, it is not a shock. He has been dead since Boise eased him out of his job. I am blaming no one. He had much going for him at one time but his own temperament was his worst enemy. I liked him.

6/10/75 I would rather have memories of Art singing "Bill Bailey" than lying dead in a casket, so didn't join the viewers.

2/9/76 He talks about death, occasionally and has me convinced that he is unafraid. I tell myself that I am the same way, so why doubt him?

3/25/76 The minister referred to him as "Clarence". I expected the coffin lid to pop open on that one!

1/3/78 The country full of sophisticated machinery that helps detect every problem in man <u>but</u> then what do you do? Maybe Dr. Hvoslef was right - why not die a natural death?

1/13/78 H.H. Humphrey died and TV full of eulogies - well earned. I never voted for him but he gained a lot of my respect over period of years. Said Mondale "He taught us how to live and taught us how to die."

5/1/78 The priest chanted impersonal prayers, repeated by mourners. Lois' name never mentioned. I wasn't concerned, feeling that God would know her without any outside help.

7/29/79 I didn't have the heart (or guts) to tell him that Wayne Judy and Don Johnson had many times discussed death and agreed that when the time came we - and all mankind - would go into oblivion even as the ducks we shot or the fish we caught.

2/11/84 She was going to a class at RRCC. The subject - Death and Dying. She should be an expert on the subject by the time our turn comes.

12/18/85 I knew him well. I can visualize him dropping a firecracker under St. Peter's robe at the Pearly Gate.

4/22/86 Fred MacKellar used to say "I have only one prayer, that I die before Irene." I know what he meant.

9/2/86 Old age is hell and the only way to beat it is to die.

Chapter 18 – Food & Things

- *One of the few things about Layna that drove Don to distraction was her inability to get rid of things.*

4/18/53 There are times when I feel that the things we have accumulated - and practically discarded, are actually smothering the life out of me.

2/11/54 Wonder if we will buy something we can't afford - even tho it is a thousand dollar item for 50 cents.

12/6/55 Goddamn but I just don't seem to beat Layna on this "gathering" business. We got a good bargain on some stuff but the hell with it, says I. Is there no point in life where we can call it quits?

3/3/59 We went over and took a look at Dahlberg's cruiser. The Queen of Rainy Lake is a broken down crone now. The kids have stripped every movable piece of brass off her. Even the lights and horn are gone. A heavy fall of snow on the boathouse roof will bury her in a mass of rotten shingles. What a pity!

10/11/62 It is never a question as to "What shall we throw away", it is always "Where shall we put it?".

10/22/65 My big job is to keep from spouting off too much on the subject, tho God knows my last 96 blow ups have had no effect. We gather and gather.

4/8/67 On to landing where a big dog just finished eating our steak and chicken from the groceries left there. He wasn't a bit frightened or sorry. He was so damned much at ease that I did not even curse him.

3/30/69 Wayne broiled venison chops on outdoor grill. I made rest of meal inside. I would have eaten the chops raw rather than stand out in that wind to cook them.

9/29/70 I feel quite certain that some of the canned goods hauled today will be eaten at my "wake".

7/10/72 Sally has baked 18 loaves of bread since coming to NWI. It goes like angel food.

12/30/72 We made mental inventory of our supplies and decided that we could live well for a month and survive for maybe 6.

2/21/73 I made one startling observation today. Our house - all of it - would fit nicely in their down stairs patio!

2/24/73 Everyone, including young priest, on to George and Maria's new house where we witnessed the blessing of the house. It took a lot of holy water.

1/19/74 A chickadee would have had poor picking on the bones

3/16/75 At one point, had I had the power, I would have breathed life into him and let him go. Now he is skinned, cut up, wrapped and in freezer. It would take a lot of money to get him from me now.

1/20/76 On to Lincoln Dells where we had the poorest Margaritas of all time but followed by a superb cheese cake which evened thing up.

7/20/76 Layna treated to scones and tea which our visitors said were just like in England - at least that is what everyone agreed they said later. As for me, I understood hardly a word.

8/31/76 To eat at place recommended by clerk and it was less than poor. We can't win them all.

1/11/79 On to mall to do some shopping - mostly for me. As Quig used to say, "I am all ragged out!"

11/27/79 I also bought a tackle box for $20.00 - the first one bought in my life. Kooch-i-ching, Dahlbergs, M & O and ADM furnished the others. Not bad.

6/20/80 If, and when, we give up this island, the little rowboat will be one of the tougher items to part with.

9/9/80 An old saying says, "You never miss the water until the well goes dry". Well, that goes for electric power, too. How did we get along without it in the "olden days"?

8/3/81 Burned up a couple of old wooden ladders. One of them, used to get in attic, was built by Chris Oien in 1927. Nothing lasts forever. Even a ladder and it's maker.

8/12/81 A new first at NWI. They brought fish for supper at $4.50 per pound. How far the mighty (me) have fallen!

11/28/81 We went to the mall to join others caught in the wave of Xmas shopping. It was a half hearted attempt - non productive.

2/22/82 In keeping with our "no alone" policy for me, Layna talked Jim Froehlich into sitting with me while she went to buy me a swimming suit, incidentally, the first one in my 75 years.

4/13/84 Dahlberg's Bee Gee, a 26 foot mahogany hull with a 165 hp inboard cost $7500 in 1927.

7/23/84 Layna to town and came home with description of devastation wrought by sewer project at 265 [mainland house]. She said, "I feel like I have been raped!"

1/5/85 The little Mazda (with 145,000 miles on it) ran thru the snow like it was having fun.

2/4/85 A good thing that Deer Island was well named. We had plenty of meat.

Chapter 19 – Money

- *Although I never knew a time when our family was short of money, practically never carrying any debt, my parents were clearly products of the depression and had a conservative relationship to money.*

4/7/52 To Norway Island with load of groceries - 4 cardboard boxes at National Tea for $49.44!

12/13/58 This is my 14th diary. Somewhere in each of the others can be found my comments on our financial standing. I am sure that in each case, I was worried about the future. It is a normal reaction, surely, and I try not to carry it to extremes. In most cases, the comments must have been brought out because of a blow-up with Layna. It seems that I have to pop off at least once a year. Generally I get everyone feeling miserable for the rest of that day. I even draw tears out of Layna, which don't come easy. I feel one of those outbursts coming on right now. I have made all kinds of mental resolutions to attack this problem calmly and with great reason. Watch for tomorrow's edition!

12/14/58 Much to my amazement, I was able to talk over our finances with Layna without getting mad. Not so amazing is the fact that we solved nothing.

7/28/64 Sally and Jim making big decisions too. They have bought a home in Minneapolis for $23,000 - taxes to be $600 a year. And you think you have problems, Old Man Johnson!

7/15/66 It must be hell to be on a job you hate that bad. Money is a great incentive

11/18/69 Don Thomas came to put new blower motor in furnace. As Layna said "We didn't need to leave home to spend $50.00 today.

8/9/71 Goddamn - they sure don't think like we do - and who is to criticize? Some people must get the same thrill out of saving a buck as I do at shooting a duck or catching a bass.

3/19/72 I don't understand these people and their regard for money. He haggled over a few pesos and then told me he made $8000.00 on a 16 month land deal.

6/4/72 She had considered having Bernice help her but her price of $2.00 an hour rather steep. Another case of a seller pricing herself out of a market.

12/6/72 We pay more and more for goods and services and both get poorer and poorer. I sometimes think that is our #1 problem, over pollution, taxes, integration, etc.

12/7/72 Much talk about wills and estates. None of us know much about it. I am certain of one thing. We at least have heirs we are happy to leave our money to. He faces the gloomy prospect of Margaret getting his!

4/6/73 We had more money coming in while we were gone than we spent, which means we are more sound that the government.

3/27/74 He wants to take two lake trout with them because fish is 3 or 4 dollars a pound in Florida!

5/6/74 They are conservative with their money - no - damned tight!

10/16/74 Wayne was kidding us about spending too much money on licenses. He didn't buy one. I said "Ya, but look what we are saving on shotgun shells".

1/19/76 I bought Sylvia Porter's *Money Book*. Hope I learn enough from it to get back the $16.00 I paid for it.

2/25/76 For many years I have known that I should get help from Marie on our income tax but afraid she will leak out information. I still feel that way after tonight's session - not that our affairs are that important!

1/4/77 Had a piece of pie at Jim's Eat Shop. $.65, coffee $.30. That knocks hell out of a buck.

3/16/77 Home at 8:30 to a rather cold house. We are trying to conserve on fuel. It makes sense to be patriotic when kerosene is $.49 a gallon.

3/14/78 I thought it rather paradoxical that he should stand in a $300,000 church (est.) looking over a $3000 (est.) casket and belittle worldly goods. Am I cynical? Yes!

4/30/79 I tried to discourage her but she insisted. What should an old man do with what he firmly believes is a bum idea? And $850.00 worth.

2/1/80 Walked down to big market. Three weeks ago we paid 60 pesos for a chicken. Today it was 78. Don't know if it is inflation or if our butcher saw the gringos coming.

8/7/80 Layna and I to Piggly Wiggly to replenish our scanty food supply. $60.00, 5 paper bags - did it. I can remember when $60.00 would buy a grub stake for the winter - for our family of 5.

8/25/80 We went to Sheridan, and after a great deal of number changing, we bought a new Chevy Citation. It cost a much as our #265 home - so goes inflation.

12/11/82 They have planned their lives well. There is one fly in the ointment. Who and where are the heirs?

1/7/83 [Going out of business sale.] Layna bought a scratch pad for $.36. At that rate no one in this generation will see that store empty.

3/11/83 We were with Karen Skifstads for about an hour and came away feeling pretty secure. I can afford to break another leg.

2/11/85 He asked for $10.00 last time so we gave him $10.00 today. Down deep I thot that it was scandalous until he said that he had paid $8.00 for a pizza. Then I heard on the news that Kent Hrbek had signed a 5 year contract for $6,000,000. We couldn't afford to have him shovel our roof.

1/18/86 The potential prizes many millions of dollars. I can't imagine anything worse than to win one of those prizes.

4/2/86 We are so damned dumb that we have soaked our future in CD's at the local bank. No wonder I was peed off - pure envy.

5/22/87 Dr. Terry Kalar started the job on my teeth. He pulled 4 and said come back next Wednesday. The estimate says the bill will be about $1400. It seems a shame to put that much money in an old head at this stage of the game.

6/8/87 Sally hard at it. She takes time off now and again for some serious discussion. Good head. John has had a few days at Curtice Island. I hope that the $6.50 an hour that he gets does not affect his future.

Chapter 20 – Religion & Spirituality

- *Both of Don's parents .were immigrants from Sweden, his mother from landed gentry and his father from the servant class. This may have colored his attitude toward religion.*

4/20/45 Sally surprised hell out of me by giving her views on religion. Those bigoted bastards in Ranier have converted her to the strongest kind of fundamentalism.

4/13/52 Newspapers tell of a tremendous surge in USA toward Christianity but so far we are not affected by it. I have not been able to accept much of what goes with being a church member and have had the courage of my convictions enough to pass same on to children. None of them baptized but an average lot morally none the less.

2/10/54 Long discussion on religion - the first time I ever let her know of my agnostic beliefs. She is old enough to know that in the battle for religious freedom, man should have the same right on not believing as he has of believing as he sees fit, and to the dictates of his own conscience.

12/16/54 A fine pair of Christians - I am afraid it is mostly talk with them!

4/19/55 I still doubt the existence of a personal God who would inflict such suffering on any of his creatures. My God is much too big for such sadistic actions.

3/22/56 Everyone is a suffering sinner to her. Well, I disagree. We may be sinners but certainly haven't suffered much for a long time.

6/6/57 Priest gave usual grave side sermon. "There he lies and you shall surely follow. Mend your ways and come to church before it is too late." I still feel that God will use his own good judgment without being influenced by the prayers of man.

4/5/59 People going to church must have thot I was nuts to be out in such weather. I wasn't too sure of their sanity, either.

6/21/59 I am afraid that under those same circumstances, I would follow the thinking of my Norseman ancestors and decide to try and make a deal with the devil.

7/24/60 Morehead said that Duffy had to attend a "Kennedy rally" meaning Mass!

12/9/60 I am a poor Mason. I try to see things objectively and for the life of me can not observe where the Masonic ritual is better than the Catholic, or Lutheran, for that matter. There is so much gobbledygook in all of them that the true meaning is smothered.

6/15/62 When he left, I told John "There is a lot about their religion that I can't go for, but men like that are what have given it much of its strength".

11/17/64 The Mormon Elders here at 8 p.m. They are working hard at a hopeless job. I told them as much but they said if we would only listen, they would keep coming to preach us the "truth". I have a hard time blaming God for the mess that is being made by the 800 religions spreading his "word".

12/5/64 ....on Mormonism - in questioning us at end of lecture, Cazier said "They you agree that man is the finest work of God." I answered, "You said that, I did not. Have you ever seen a hummingbird fly up to a flower, draw the nectar, back away and on to the next. He also can fly non-stop across the Gulf of Mexico. Don Johnson can't do that!"

2/6/65 Reverend Saunders gave a good talk for a preacher.

3/19/65 Letter from Beryl. A tearjerker for sure. Raymond dying by inches. Can't swallow. Where is our merciful God?

6/15/68 The faith that he preaches on Sunday does not apply to something as earthly as a marriage. In God we trust, but not in one another!

11/2/68 The minister droned on and on and it was with great difficulty that I kept awake. I kept thinking "If Fred were alive he would say 'For Christ sake, get on with the show!'"

11/3/68 As we drove along Ponema Point we passed many Indian graves which consisted of a rough box sitting on stilts about a foot high. George commented on the "pagan" custom. I asked him what he thot one of these pagans would say if he saw a $2000 casket lowered into the cold, cold ground.

12/16/68 I told her "If anyone says anything to me, I will say that we were able to accept Robin, even tho he did have a minister in the family."

11/9/69 I feel very strongly that Grace Davey, certainly the epitome of a true Christian lady, is just as dead as the deer our boys shot yesterday, with no after life but in the memories of those who loved her.

1/22/70 I still have trouble believing there is a god who is interested in the doings of Don Johnson as long as there are such bigger problems to be solved.

1/23/70 As Margaret asked forgiveness for our sins I thot, "My greatest sin at the moment is my lack of faith. I do believe, however, that if God is listening in, he will forgive that one."

3/14/70 Well, maybe it is true that life is for the living. Of one thing I am certain. The people who say that immortality consists of the memories (good deeds) that one leaves behind are all wet. It is short lived at best.

4/28/70 Took Bertrand Russell's *Unpopular Essays* to bed with me. Wanted something to put me to sleep. It did not work. Many of his views, especially about religion, I have arrived at myself, I think independently. It is gratifying to know that someone else does not think that Man is God's greatest work.

7/25/70 Layna and I in for Janet Burrock's wedding. The damned priest droned on for more than an hour. I awoke now and then to see others nodding so it wasn't just me.

8/4/70 A short service, maybe the minister knew, as did most of the mourners, that in life Billy Martin did not believe one damned word said.

9/7/70 I can't conceive of a mind such as Dick Nelson's having such a strong rapport with God. It must prove that there is something wrong with my thinking - but what?

11/1/70 George to church - I told him that he would never live long enough to make restitution for his sins but he has the Catholic happy philosophy that all will be well by going to mass.

11/9/70 All well and we took off for Rev. Nelson's for dinner. Fine people for sure - and Christians! They are the best kind of influence on our kids.

2/11/71 It is very difficult for us to understand a mentality that comes to Mexico and tries to woo the peons away from Catholicism.

5/19/71 It is great for theologians to tell of their feeling of inferiority when they view the grand works of the Creator. I get this feeling most when I stand and admire some of the works of my fellowmen.

6/7/71 I did not think about asking the Reverend to say grace until we were almost thru. I then thot, "This is our house, we don't say it when we are alone, why now?" and felt better.

11/30/71 Charity (and religion) should begin at home. I think that a true Christian would give his own parents a little more thought.

4/18/72 We old-uns will drop off one at a time till we are all gone - to be replaced by what are young-uns now. We are no more important then the trees which follow the same cycle.

10/18/72 We, immediate family, were herded into a stuffy little room where we heard service thru microphone speaker. It could well have been a recording, it was so impersonal. On to cemetery where we could identify voice at graveside service. Knowing what Warren thought of it all (religion), I had to feel it was all a sham, which it will be when I go.

6/12/73 I knew it would be a tough assignment alone but the commencement speaker last Sunday said that that was the only way to attain fulfillment.

7/5/73 Daily quote in diary book "Fear always springs from ignorance" - Emerson

Added below it "So does valor" - D. Johnson

9/6/73 He asked me point blank if I believed in a hereafter and I told him "no'. Tried not to elaborate. I would hate to shake his faith, even a little bit.

12/24/73 The professional Christians don't get along any better than the amateurs - and not as well as some heathens.

5/27/74 Some time ago read of story of Christian in lion's den praying and elated to see that lion was praying, too. Not so happy when he learned that lion was saying grace!

3/12/75 Home to read from Bible, not because I caught religion, but to check up on things the Pastor had said. He will never land me!

5/7/75 I can't recall when I was more concerned about anything. At one time, when a huge flow hit the end piling and the whole structure shuddered, I involuntarily looked heavenward and almost prayed. I quickly realized that God had much more important matters to attend to than Don Johnson and his dock. However, this does indicate how desperate I was.

12/6/75 No religious talk, altho Dennis told about small prayer he had said just before the Lord sent him a nice buck to shoot last fall.

1975 Special Data: Clair Huffaker - "The Cowboy & the Cossack" page 111. "I believe that people who are devoutly religious, within any specific religion, have no true respect for the ultimate vastness that is God."

11/22/77 Learned much about her including fact that she has the makings of a "Bible freak". Full of predictions of calamities to come. Cheerful otherwise.

1/17/78 Lois Beyers to see me for a half hour. A good Catholic, full of faith, but willing to talk (and well) to this heathen. Reverend

Schumacher dropped in. Good company. He, too, knows my religion, and so far hasn't shunned me.

12/20/78 Finished Moberg's *The Settlers*. A good study on my Swedish ancestry. It gave me a good insight as to why my mother was so religious - and why my father was not.

3/4/79 Many testimonials on wall from people cured by prayer. Are we happier for not believing (having faith) in such goings on?

4/14/79 When I asked her what her plans were for the summer, she said "I have none. I have decided to let Jesus lead me and I will go where he says." I almost asked about all the other decisions in past years but realized I should stay out of that kind of a discussion. Is it because I don't want to say anything to upset our friendship or am I afraid of what she might tell me?

4/18/79 Here is a quote from a copy of a letter I wrote Marcellus Murdock of the "Wichita Eagle" 8/8/46. "The book *Change Your Life by Prayer* came yesterday -----. I know that my life was changed considerably by not praying so am interested in knowing what might have been."

6/16/79 All the Catholics are praying for sunshine tomorrow. Can't miss, because I sent out a few with my "unfamiliar voice".

10/19/79 She says she will not accept the new Susan B. Anthony dollars because she heard that Sue was an atheist.

12/18/79 She is a good looking gal and apparently quite religious. We don't hold that against her.

Special Data 1979 "The gloom of the world is but a shadow; behind it, yet, within our reach, is joy. Take joy!" Fra Giovanni AD 1513 *Tasha Tudor Book*

10/18/80 She had her Subaru. We went for a ride and when I said that I thought she had made a wise choice, she said it was God's will that she buy it! She was dead serious. She went on to tell about her retired father who was an alcoholic and became abusive when drinking. A real problem. I did not have nerve enough to inquire if that was God's will, too.

12/3/80 We got into some heavy conversation on religion. Not very productive because we think too much alike, therefore no arguments.

12/16/80 Reverend Harold Schumacher officiated and true to the Lutheran tradition, he had his doubts if Katie would pass through the pearly gates - this despite the fact that she loved her friends, her flowers and fed the birds. She did not go to church. He choked up badly several times. I can only guess why.

4/19/81 Another Easter Sunday with no religious overtones by the elder Johnsons. Heathen, Pagan, Agnostic, you name it and it could fit.

6/30/81 She thanked us for our prayers, which led me to think- as Father Upson said "the Lord quite often is attentive to an unfamiliar voice".

7/17/81 She knows that Jesus is real and on her side. I wouldn't start anything with that pair.

10/8/82 The church full of well-wishers. The priest full of advice.

10/13/82 It was followed by an evangelist who was not as rabid as some TV preachers. There was a faint odor of sulfur and brimstone in the church when he finished.

3/16/83 Much religion talk, but it doesn't bother us when it comes from her.

4/3/83 Fern Laurion was once asked if she attended church regularly and her answer was only at Christmas, Easter and New Years so she could "see the whores, pimps and taxicab drivers".

8/31/83 She is a good thinker, not necessarily an attribute in a minister.

11/20/84 A natural gas storage tank blew up in Mexico City. Estimated dead - 400. Hundreds more badly injured. Thousands homeless. God's will?

1/23/86 I am afraid to discuss religion with a pro. I am so comfortable with my beliefs and I don't want them upset.

2/9/86 At the moment I think that I wouldn't mind going every Sunday but I am afraid I would start tongues wagging "Don Johnson joined the church. He is worried about his 80 years!"

2/16/86 The narrator said repeatedly, "God didn't plan for man to go hungry". If that is true, He has lost command! The minister invited anyone who accepted Jesus Christ to come forth and join the church. I wasn't ready and seriously doubt if I ever will be.

2/15/87 To church. I don't know exactly why. I guess it must be to please Layna. I am not trying to build up brownie points at this late stage of the game.

4/8/87 She hopes to do like Karen, get a church and settle down. If the trend continues, I may live to learn that God is female. "Our Mother, who art in heaven - - -."

4/17/87 In talking about the loose morals of the populace, she declared that she was a 40 year old virgin and proud of it. I wasn't shocked, only a little surprised to hear her tell it.

Chapter 21 - Self

- *This is a chapter that is probably as self explanatory as any. I have little more to add.*

11/9/48 Spent much of morning browsing around in downtown stores. NUTS! Never could see any sense in city life, and can see less now.

10/14/49 I am irritable as hell. Must be a strain on me being nice to people for so long. Looks like it doesn't come naturally - or maybe it is expecting too much of flesh and bones!

3/5/50 Wonder what would have to happen in my life to give me a superiority complex!

6/25/50 Much card playing and drinking. The foulest language imaginable. I am far from sensitive but at times it is getting me down.

8/18/50 To town for first time in many a day and I don't care when I go back again.

10/7/51 .... and excellent company. I surely expand in that environment. I think clearer, express myself better. It makes me feel that I could have gone places in almost any field - and still no regrets. I like the one I am in! (cocky bastard!)

5/7/52 I am pretty miserable tonight - don't know what I would do without Layna to keep my spirits up.

5/11/52 I honestly think they made special trip to razz me about hitting rock. I must be a real important man in these parts when something like that makes such a furor. As usual, reports greatly exaggerated - but somehow over as period of years, I have built up a great resistance for such things - and I'm not badly hurt.

11/25/52 No power on earth or money incentive either, could make me live and operate in the center of that hubbub. [Chicago]

12/21/52 Cut Xmas tree and had usual trouble finding what we wanted. Same as anything else in life - always trouble when so great a choice afforded.

1/10/53 A year from now, I'll either say "Why in hell didn't I do this before?" or else "What in hell was I thinking about to spend all that money?!"

11/23/53 Jesus Christ, what a day! At one time I was ready to commit arson, suicide or both. One damned minor (and major) irritant until I was about nuts. Thank the Lord for Layna. She always brings me back to what might be called an even keel. Went to bed in disgust at 9:30. Woke up at 12 and tossed for ½ hour and then got up. Went to work for 2 hours and really accomplished something. Back to sleep up at 6 a.m.

2/1/54 "Many people seek eternity who don't know what to do with themselves on a rainy afternoon."

2/9/54 The human system has great adaptability but I seriously doubt if I could (or would want to) live without her.

4/25/54 I know damned well I went to a daytime show today to duck company.

5/11/54 Right now, I feel as tho I have been navigation uncharted seas in a leaky boat, and altho I have been pumping manfully for some time, am about to go down with the ship.

5/14/54 Much has changed - mostly me, I suppose, and most for the better. For sure my feet are more firmly on the ground. The problem now is not to let them get there so firmly that they take root.

7/13/54 It looks like we are all getting what we want, an unusual situation.

2/26/55 I was resentful only once, when I gazed at the wonders of sporting equipment at Abercrombie. The customers, for the most part, were big shots, buying things that I wanted but could not afford. I then thot of the Natural History Museum where my capacity for enjoyment surpassed theirs, and felt better.

7/4/55 I am too poor to enjoy luxury of getting impatient over anything, let alone a few minutes wait.

3/8/56 These minor ecstasies are a matter of degree. I probably feel as good about my poem as Milton did over "Paradise Lost". Probably better - he was blind and sour!

3/27/56 As far as I am concerned we are dealing with a basic human failing and are in no position to change it.

9/6/56 The older I get the more I realize that the most contemptible failing in human nature is that of ingratitude.

9/20/57 I towed him to Water Narrows, but not before I swamped most of outfit and formed a pretty poor opinion of Canadian Wardens in general.

10/1/58 It is easy to be generous when one has so much. I am sure that is the basic philosophy behind most philanthropy.

12/5/58 People take too damned much for granted and would rather have their tongues torn out than say a pleasant word to someone's face.

4/26/59 I made most philosophical statement. Said that the trouble with square dancers is that they are people first and dancers after.

6/1/59 This definitely one of our better days, and one to think about when thing get tough - as they are sure to do.

12/11/59 By the time a man is 40, he is what he is and if he hasn't learned those lessons by then, fine words won't do the trick.

1/18/60 It is poor sport to take pot shots at the same target as all the rest of the self styled experts.

1/8/61 I feel badly about the whole business, but either too lazy or cautious to stir deeper into the crap for fear of making a stronger smell. I am not proud of it.

1/14/61 I must be having menopause to let myself get so damned upset!

12/31/61 So endeth another year and the 17th of these little books. There are a few blank pages in all of them - literally - and no doubt more figuratively. By and large, they give a fair account of the activities of me and mine. I have had occasion to read back on some of the back issues and my chief criticism lies in the fact that too much space is given to blow by blow accounts of activities without enough given to what goes on in this bald head. Maybe just as well.

1/3/62 I guess I haven't the sternness required to be a big executive.

12/19/62 Not sleeping worth a damn - many minor irritants. Don't know what I would do if something important turned up.

1/23/63 The best course now is to read and hope to be stimulated by what I do understand and not be frustrated by what I do not.

2/7/63 One of the most satisfying of all human feelings is to be able to say "I like those people - they like me!"

4/8/63 Well, I suppose I will have a major concern (at least one at a time) as long as I live, and should be happy there are not more.

1/1/65 Here goes the 20th edition, looks like I am in a rut. By a bit of rough calculation, I came up with the following. At approximately 7000 days @ approximately 100 words per day, I have written approximately 700,000 words. That is about ½ of what Churchill wrote the first year of his retirement - and he said something. Well, he didn't have any more fun using his big brain than I did using mine. It is all relative

1/13/65 Stanley Swenson still gets on my nerves. Maybe it is because he is so goddamn sure of his every opinion and I can't make up my mind on anything. I am continuously trying to see both sides of any argument and consequently the more I think the more confused I get.

8/19/65 [Lear Jet flight] God, what an experience for a country boy! I saw no angels but feel that was as close to heaven as I'll ever get.

11/28/65 Fern brought our cat back and I can honestly say I was glad to see him. A sure sign I am getting soft in my old age.

1/27/67 I have given my Spanish lessons an all out effort all week. I can see a break thru - but it is faint and far away.

3/7/67 Cat up on table when I came home and that almost terminated a beautiful friendship.

9/11/67 I know now that one of my deeper pleasures comes from helping others do what they want to do.

7/3/68 I think we are on firmer ground, which still is shaky.

5/4/69 I missed both wars and in retrospect, I feel about the same as I do about going through the ice in a car, an experience I can live without.

6/7/69 No Jim, no Bob. Damn their Indian souls to a hunting ground where there is neither fish nor game - or squaws!

9/8/69 I try to tell myself that I don't miss the old setup but know damned well that a part of me went when we closed her up.

11/10/69 Stumbled around, tried to reappraise life in general and my own in particular but arrived at no startling conclusion.

9/5/70 Head too full to activate hands.

9/8/70 I hate garrulous old (or young) people and would not want to be classed as one. Be careful, Johnson!

11/2/70 Why is it that we all hate to show our ignorance when in reality that is what we have the most of.

1/19/71 I brought tape recorder out of basement and scratched away at the idea of taping some of the high spots of my life. I suppose I will be like Ober -I'll take it all with me.

2/26/71 An old saying goes "If you want something done, ask a busy man to do it." How true! I haven't a damned thing to do in this world other than write a letter to our kids (a job I thoroly enjoy) and I just can't seem to find the time.

4/21/71 Harry played organ and Layna and I sang "Happy Birthday" recording for Bernie. It was awful and I ended it with "Oh, S**t!"

4/27/71 I never could see why the bathroom should be the fanciest room in a home. Maybe anything looks better to me than the old "2 holers" we used for years.

12/5/71 After he left we all made fun of the way he murdered the English language. I would give much to be able to talk Spanish as well as he does English.

12/8/71 Finished up the 5 napkin holders and almost had one of my old time fits (strong urge to throw) when I discovered one was badly off center. Not sure if it was maturity or senility that stayed my hand.

12/16/71 A stranger hearing me curse and swear would call a cop. Layna takes it all very calmly, outwardly at least.

2/1/72 Goddamn, I was peed off. Layna assumed full blame but I am past the stage in life when that is important.

4/28/72 A couple of bloopers held me up. A few years ago I would have thrown hammer thru the window. Took it all rather philosophically. Maybe it is because I know myself better so don't expect too much anymore.

11/18/72 The seventh day since Layna went into the hospital. I don't like it. I am fully aware of what life would be without her - and wonder if I could face up to it.

2/12/73 What a great boon to man is his ability to forget.

2/26/73 I try not to get emotional when saying goodbye but fail miserably. Layna says not to worry about it - so I won't.

8/3/73 What a goddamn mess some people (most, I guess) make of their lives.

12/27/73 We were in a different league, full of structures, syndromes, images etc., etc., etc. Would to God there was some way to put these great ideas to practical use.

3/19/74 A combination of honesty and fear (mostly the later) made me declare it.

4/18/74 Made a cup of cocoa and drank it in the sun on main dock. Thought of life and death and decided I had two good reasons for not wanting to die. I hate to leave Layna and family - and Norway Island. I won't get anything better in the "sweet by and by."

12/5/74 In reviewing the incident with Layna later, we both thought I used a great deal of restraint. Is that good? Does it mean that I don't have any steam to let off?

4/17/75 I dilly, dallied, fiddled and farted about going to Duluth.

4/22/75 I can be a good listener when I find someone with something to say - an infrequent experience.

5/13/76 I was leading Wayne down path when he stopped and said "Goodbye, Happy Shack. I won't be back. I have had many good times here." He began to cry and it took all my self control to keep from bawling with him. Now I wish I had!

8/21/77 I try to review the summer objectively and have a hard time determining my own feelings. I realize most of all that I am changing - quite rapidly, and not for the better. It is increasingly difficult to hide my feelings. Maybe I shouldn't.

2/22/78 When writing to Osbergs, I stumbled over spelling word "Geography." I could see my 4th grade teacher, Miss Montain teaching us "George Elliot's old grandmother rode a pig home yesterday." The human memory is beyond understanding.

7/31/79 I worked out a scheme to keep from bawling at service. The pall bearers sat within touching distance of casket. It was a fine piece of workmanship and I visualized Wayne building it, knowing well that he could have done the job.

9/21/79 There are many changes in me, my attitude toward night travel on lake one of the most pronounced. I hate it.

7/3/80 I helped a little, but my heart was not in it. To tell the truth, there isn't much that my heart is in.

10/9/80 Harry and I down town to have coffee with his gang. About 14 there. At Harry's insistence, I told the Finlander bridge story. I firmly believe that I will never tell it again. That means another closed chapter in my life.

10/28/80 What a pair of articulate people. I am a pushover for anyone who expresses himself well, no matter what the subject.

12/5/81 I am amazed with my patience. I should not be. I no longer throw tools or even swear. It must be due to a gradual numbing of the senses.

6/22/82 I am so damned unsteady I would fall in for sure. I haven't reached the point where I would welcome that.

8/13/82 Much talk about Women's Lib. They tried to draw me in but I knew I was no match for such talent - with one leg, yet!

11/22/82 It is quite a struggle to be super, super careful every waking hour.

3/15/84 I must be getting mellow, because she didn't irritate me as much as usual.

7/5/85 After reading the above, I say to myself, "Who the hell cares about all of this?" I have no answer other than I am in a rut that I can't get out of.

8/20/85 They picked up the cat, and to prove I am getting senile, I hated to see it go.

2/5/86 It is confusing work and it takes a clear mind to get it straight. That is a commodity that is in short supply at #265.

1/27/86 After it was over the comment heard most was "You should write a book." How many times have I heard that line?

8/9/86 Days like the last two should be cherished for ever, and reviewed when the going gets tough.

3/11/87 At one time I thought it smart to tell stories with a Finlander accent, but that all changed when I tried to learn Spanish. I decided that I would be happy if I could speak as fluent Spanish as well as the dumbest Finn could speak English.

4/6/87 [Don's birthday] After getting in bed I laid awake for some time reliving the days activities which led me to make a short, intense, reflection of my full 81 years. It couldn't be much in detail but the main facts were sharp and clear. It has been a good life.

Made in the USA
Charleston, SC
19 May 2010